T0133217

Universität Ulm, Fakultät für Informatik
Abteilung Programmmiermethodik und Compilerbau
Leiter: Prof. Dr. Helmuth Partsch

Understanding Software Acquisition Through Modeling and Simulation

Dissertation
Zur Erlangung des Doktorgrades Dr. rer. nat.
der Fakultät für Informatik der Universität Ulm

vorgelegt von

Tobias Häberlein
aus Öhringen

2004

Amtierender Dekan:	Prof. Dr. Friedrich von Henke
1. Gutachter:	Prof. Dr. Helmuth Partsch
2. Gutachter:	Prof. Dr. Franz Schweiggert
Tag der Promotion:	8. Juni 2004

Bibliografische Information Der Deutschen Bibliothek

Die Deutsche Bibliothek verzeichnet diese Publikation in der Deutschen
Nationalbibliografie; detaillierte bibliografische Daten sind im Internet über
http://dnb.ddb.de abrufbar.

ISBN 3-8325-0601-2

Logos Verlag Berlin
Comeniushof, Gubener Str. 47,
10243 Berlin
Tel.: +49 030 42 85 10 90
Fax: +49 030 42 85 10 92
INTERNET: http://www.logos-verlag.de

Acknowledgements

I wrote this dissertaton during an employment as a research assistent at the department for "Programmiermethodik und Compilerbau". First of all, I thank the whole department. Without you lively, funny, and crazy folks, I would have become desperate from time to time of my lonesome brooding about software process simulation.

I thank my supervisor Prof. Dr. Partsch for giving me the actual sparking inspiration for this dissertation: "Why not try to simulate this acquisition process model?", he suggested during a discussion about possible research directions. He gave me the necessary freedom for realizing all my ideas. I thank my co-supervisor Prof. Dr. Schweiggert. Through his straightforward and pragmatic manner, he contributed to the successful outcome of this work.

I thank my partners at DaimlerChrysler, namely Bärbel Hörger for the financial support and Thomas Gantner for the fruitful and pleasant cooperation and the level of responsibility he trustfully put on me in doing research with him. The work with Thomas formes the basis for this dissertation.

And I thank Viktoria for believing in my abilities and encouraging me in going my way.

Contents

Contents

III. System Dynamics Simulation 87

Contents

List of Figures

Chapter 1

Introduction

The subject of software development has been treated extensively during the last 40 years in the respective literature starting with publications by Royce [70], Weinberg [84], Brook's "Mythical Man-Month" [9], and systematized voluminous software engineering books like Pressman's [62] and Sommerville's [82] textbook. Though nearly as many projects face the task of *acquiring* software from a third-party than producing software themselves, and even though there are lots of indicators showing that, in many respects, software acquisition projects are even more complex and risky than software development projects, there is quite a small amount of publications dealing with the acquisition of software from third parties compared to the vast amount of literature and research dealing with the development of software.

This work is about the rather unexplored subject of software acquisition and ways to better understand software acquisition projects, their behavior, and their underlying dynamic rules. We use both established techniques, like System Dynamics simulation which is applied in part III, and novel techniques, which have been developed in the scope of this dissertation, like the process model architecture described in part I, the process-oriented interactive simulation technique described in part II, and a combination, described in part IV, of System Dynamics simulation and the process-oriented interactive simulation.

This introductory chapter is organized as follows: section 1.1 determines, what we understand by "software acquisition", defines the terminology used in this thesis, and examines the matter of "software acquisition" in a wider context. Section 1.2 uses systems theory to sketch the particular complexity of software acquisition projects. The aims of this dissertation are explained in section 1.3, and section 1.4 gives an overview of the structure of this dissertation.

1.1. Software Acquisition

Software acquisition and supplier management are critical issues for many enterprises world-wide. Their impact on business processes is increasing dramatically. At many automotive companies, for instance, the greatest part of the business and automotive software is provided by suppliers, often developed in software acquisition projects which get increasingly complex. Therefore, tools are needed to manage process complexity and to support process improvement and assessment in acquisition projects.

After shortly sketching what we actually understand by "software acquisition" in section 1.1.1, section 1.1.2 specifies the terminology used throughout this dissertation. Section 1.1.3 examines the matter of "software acquisition" in a wide perspective – at least wider than our treatment in the rest of this dissertation – with the help of Williamson's Transaction Cost Theory.

1.1.1. What is Software Acquisition?

Software acquisition is concerned with the purchase of software. Acquisition projects are comparatively simple when the organization's demand can be met by a standard COTS[1] product. COTS software products are readily available and frequently sold products which have solely to be parameterized and integrated into an existing infrastructure. If integration becomes too complex, however, a custom-made software product is often the better choice.

This work deals with acquisition projects for custom-made software products. Compared to COTS procurement, these projects are harder to manage and more risky. To find an appropriate supplier, a well managed tender procedure should be performed. After providing the (often immature) requirements to the supplier, the supplier's development project starts. Changing requirements, the supplier's problems, and contract changes should be communicated, and the supplier's progress should be monitored and controlled to get a predictable outcome.

1.1.2. Terminology

There is no common definition of the term "Software acquisition". We shortly compare the definition of "Software acquisition" due to different sources and finally present the meaning of "Software acquisition" used in this work.

---

[1] "COTS" is an abbreviation for "Commercial-off-the-shelf"

Terminology in other Work

Meyers and Oberndorf [54] define "procurement" to be the actual process of purchasing the software and "software acquisition" to be the whole process around the purchasing, including procurement:

> "[Software acquisition is ...] the set of activities performed to procure, develop, and maintain a system. However, some might limit the term 'acquisition' to procurement only, but we feel that such a view is too narrow. Acquisition is much more than simply procurement activities. Projects need to understand development and maintenance activities in order to succeed in procurement aspects of acquisition."

Due to ISO/IEC 12207 [43] the purpose of the software acquisition process is:

> "[...] to obtain the product and/or service that satisfies the need expressed by the customer. The process begins with the identification of a customer need and ends with the acceptance of the product and/or service needed by the customer."

and the software acquisition process subdivides into the steps "Acquisition Preparation", "Supplier Selection", "Supplier Monitoring", and "Customer Acceptance".

PULSE [64] defines "software acquisition" to be

> "[...] the processes of acquiring an ICT product [i.e. an Information and Communication Technology product] and generally all activities that are undertaken by the acquirer during the entire acquisition life cycle".

And, like in the aforementioned definitions of Meyers and Oberndorf, PULSE defines "procurement" to a sub-activity of acquisition: "[procurement is ...] the range of activities associated with contracting the delivery of an ICT product as seen and managed by the acquirer. Procurement is one part of the acquisition process".

Terminology Used in this Work

We focus on the acquirer's perspective. The activities conducted by the supplier are of secondary interest in this work. We treat "pure" software acquisition projects, i.e. we assume that there are no development activities by the acquirer himself; it is solely the supplier who designs the software and implements the programming code. Furthermore, when speaking of "software acquisition" we mean the procurements of custom-made software products; we leave the procurement of COTS software products aside. Therefore, except of part III where we use a more restricted definition, we understand the following by the term "software acquisition":

Definition 1.1 (Software Acquisition) *The set of all possible activities which need to be performed by the acquirer in order to contract and procure a software system (particularly, a custom-made software system) from a third party, and to integrate it in the existing IT environment.*

We generally avoid using the term "procurement", and we always – also in part III – use the term "software acquisition" to name the process of buying software from third parties.

We also avoid using the confusing term "customer" – at least confusing in the context of software acquisition; some use the term "customer" to name the acquirer, some use the term "customer" to name the project or organization that buys the software from the acquirer. We stick to the two terms "acquirer" and "supplier" which are frequently used throughout this dissertation:

Definition 1.2 (Acquirer) *The project / organizational unit that prepares the request for proposal, selects the supplier, monitors and controls the supplier, and finally accepts the software product.*

Definition 1.3 (Supplier) *The project / organizational unit (which could even be part of the acquirer's organization) developing and delivering the software product(s) to the acquirer.*

Some books and standards use the term "contractor" with a similar meaning. But we solely use "supplier" to name the organization which develops and delivers the software product.

1.1.3. Software Acquisition in a Wider Perspective: Williamson's Transaction Cost Theory

In his transaction cost theory [86], Williamson mainly treats the question which motivations bring an organization to outsource the development of special products or services. Lacity and Hirschheim [47] utilize this theory for reasoning about outsourcing information systems (whereas the central topic of this dissertation, namely outsourcing the development of *custom-made* software products, is just a special case thereof) and particularly for reasoning about the question under which circumstances information systems outsourcing is reasonable for a given organization, and for reasoning about the dangers and annoyances in the decision to outsource. This dissertation focuses on the question how to best manage a project *after* an organization or organizational unit came to the decision to outsource. But nevertheless, sketching the answers to *all* these questions is important to get a view on the subject of software acquisition as a whole. Furthermore, Williamson's transaction cost theory provides interesting insights on the relevance of certain aspects of the software acquisition process, particularly aspects – like the importance of reasonable monitoring and controlling mechanisms or proper communication between acquirer and supplier – which this dissertation focuses on in later chapters, and so we present some of Williamson's ideas here.

Why do organizations decide to outsource the development of a software product instead of developing it on their own? Williamson's view is that organizational members make outsourcing decisions mainly base on economic rationale; they are trying to optimize costs. His theory treats not only *production costs* but also *transaction costs*, i.e. the costs for coordination, monitoring, controlling, and managing transactions. Assessing costs, however, is often difficult and Williamson's primary construct are the following heuristics to assess costs:

- *Transaction types*: There are two aspects worth mentioning here: a high frequency decreases the production costs and a high *asset specificity* increases the production costs. Custom-made software products are probably the most asset-specific artifacts existing, and their production costs tend to be high compared to the transaction costs emerging from outsourcing their development; this is one reason why many organizations which demand software decide to buy rather than make.

- *Threat of opportunism*: Williamson notes that, under certain conditions, the transaction costs can be substantial if the vendor (i.e. the supplier in the case of software acquisition) behaves *opportunistically* – he extends the meaning that people act on their own self-interest to "self-interest with guile". His theory claims that a market with a large number of suppliers minimizes this threat. In the case of outsourcing the development of custom-made software, opportunism is often no problem at the beginning of a project when choosing the supplier. However, it becomes a problem in the course of the acquisition:

the supplier gains knowledge about the product and respective domain and, thereby, he gains advantage over possible competitors, and this, in turn, effectively minimizes the number of possible suppliers. Thus, there is a great threat of opportunism and a resulting threat of increased transaction costs when the supplier is well-established. According to Williamson, there is one way to mitigate the threat of opportunism in this case: setting up appropriate controlling and monitoring structures. Part III deals mainly with this crucial aspect of software acquisition.

- *Uncertainty*: Williamson notes that transactions are conducted under uncertainty when it is very costly or even impossible to describe the complete decision tree for the course of the project. Particularly for asset-specific investments, like the acquisition of custom-made software products from third parties, uncertainty increases transaction costs substantially. According to Williamson, such projects need

  > "[...] a machinery to work things out since contractual gaps will be larger and the occasions for sequential adaptions will increase in number and importance as the degree of uncertainty changes." [85], page 254

  This again emphasizes the importance of a controlling and monitoring "machinery" for successful acquisition projects.

The consequences from Williamson's transaction cost theory for our view on the acquisition of custom-made software products can be summed up to the following points:

- It is, in many cases, profitable for a company *not* to develop asset-specific custom-made software products internally but to outsource their development. This explains the great number of software projects dealing solely with the acquisition of software products. This is especially true for domains where very specialized products are needed like in industries demanding embedded software (e.g. the automotive industry). The case studies used in this dissertation (see chapter 3 and 8) stem from the automotive industry.

- Mechanisms for monitoring and controlling the supplier are crucial to the success of acquisition projects. In fact, parts of this dissertation, namely chapter 7 and chapter 8, focus on exactly this aspect of the software acquisition process.

1.2. Complexity of Software Acquisition Projects

Software *development* projects, especially those which run many months and which involve lots of people, are hard to manage; many things can go wrong and often actually go wrong. The fact that many people with many (in)abilities must be coordinated to work on an issue that is immaterial, complex, and thus highly error-prone, makes this kind of projects so intricate. Software *acquisition* projects seem to be even less understood than pure software development projects. Not only must the work of the acquisition project's staff be coordinated, which is by itself already difficult and often does not work smoothly, but also the more sumptuous inter-project coordination with the suppliers is needed, and – to cap it all – the suppliers work on the error-prone issue of software.

There is a recent tendency to measure the scientific maturity of any discipline with its ability not to reduce the complexity of its particular subject but to seriously treat that complexity and develop techniques to deal with it. Systems theory is a discipline independent way to deal with complexity [87]. We utilize a systems theoretic view on acquisition projects in this section. The causes of acquisition's particular complexity can be illustrated well thereby.

Figure 1.1 shows the *causal loop diagram* of a project from a very high-

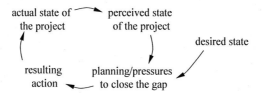

Figure 1.1.: Generic causal loop diagram of a project

level viewpoint. It illustrates the causal structures of projects regardless of their type, size, involved products, or any other specific characteristics. In fact, if we would simply replace the term "project" in figure 1.1 by the term "system", it may even serve as a generic view on *every* system. The arcs – they are called "causal-links" – indicate that there exists some kind of causal relationship or influence of one state on another. So, the picture says that the actual state of the project influences the way the state of the project is perceived. Pressures and appropriate planning result, in order to close the gap between the perceived state of the project and the desired state (which is derived amongst other things from schedule plans, budget demands, and external requirements). The resulting action takes effect on the actual state of the project, which again influences the perceived state, and so on. Here we have a closed sequence of causes and effects, a closed path of action and information, which is usually called *feedback loop*. The reader may wonder, why the actual state of the project is not compared directly with the desired state. It is characteristic for system sciences, especially for system dynamics modeling, to differentiate between "actual" facts and facts how they are perceived by the system's agents. And in fact, it is realistic to assume that fallible human agents are not able to objectively perceive the reality. Figure 1.1 shows a *negative* feedback loop, or "goal-seeking" loop. Such loops are trying to find an equilibrium (here, the loop seeks to adapt the perceived state of the project to the desired state); positive feedback loops, in contrast, are destabilizing, self-reinforcing, or growth-producing – they are often experienced as vicious circles. System sciences assume that feedback structures are the main determinants of the behavior of a system.

After this sketchy excursion into system sciences, let's have a look how acquisition projects can be described in systems theory's view. Compared to pure in-house ventures, there is a further level of indirection intrinsic to acquisition: like in software development projects, acquisition projects adhere to the typical project dynamics: we have to perceive the staff's progress, compare it to the desired progress, and react accordingly. But the fact that the actions of the acquisition's staff are – at least partially, when it comes to the monitoring and controlling of the supplier – *controlling* development and thus managerial by their nature makes acquisition more intricate; compared to development projects, we have to deal with one additional "actual state → perceived state → resulting pressures"-loop. Figure 1.2 shows this through a causal loop diagram.

There is another, but similar, reasonable angle to view the cause of higher complexity. In addition to the "perceive"-variables, we have to deal with a second source of subjectiveness: variables expressing the status *reported* by the supplier; figure 1.3 shows this additional source of subjectiveness in bold face. For obvious reasons, the "subjective" variables have no simple cause and effect relationships but are highly enmeshed with the rest of the system and are therefore the most relevant sources for intricate and unpredictable behavior. The reported state is obviously influenced by the actual state of the project, but there are many more factors which affect it: the reported state not only depends on the supplier's ability to correctly perceive the state (and thus by its management skills) but also on the supplier's attitude towards the acquirer, on his trust, and on his general mindset towards the

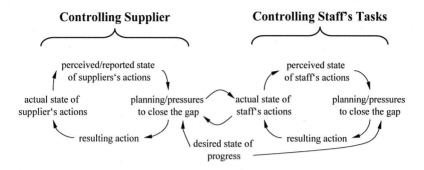

Figure 1.2.: The two controlling loops of the acquisition process.

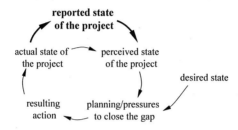

Figure 1.3.: Additional element in the project loop of acquisition.

project. Things get even more complicated, if we consider how the acquirer builds his picture of the project's state. So, dealing with just one further root of subjectiveness entails a dramatic growth in behavior complexity.

The more complex a project is, the more subtle are the tools needed for supporting the project participants. The aims of this dissertation are closely related with the design of such supportive tools for software acquisition projects

1.3. Aims of this Work

As illustrated in the last section, software acquisition projects are complex and risky. On the other hand, according to established literature about software acquisition [47, 54, 67] and according to the author's experience[2],

---

[2]The author coorporates with a software research center of an automotive company, and in this context he consults software acquisition projects in the area of process

both management and technical staff members often underestimate the complexity of software acquisition projects and understand too less about their dynamics: the requirements given to the supplier are often incomplete, the supplier is not well-chosen, the customer-supplier communication is poor and sometimes simply not existing, and there is too less monitoring of the supplier in most acquisition projects. An important issue, thus, is, first, to illustrate problematic behavior in acquisition projects and, second, to raise awareness about the complexity inherent in acquisition projects and the need to mitigate the respective risks.

The direction of the research presented in this dissertation is based on the assumption that there is already enough information material, suggestions, and best practices about software acquisition in textbook form. This textbook material, though surely reasonable and based on many valuable experiences in the field of software acquisition, affects project managers and project members quite little when they are stressed with everyday project life; a software acquisition textbook is just another document on the desks of busy managers. This dissertation rather concentrates on alternative methods to impart knowledge about the dynamics of software acquisition projects and establishes techniques supporting non-textbook-style learning.

We conclude to delimit this work by noting what the aims are *not*. This dissertation primarily discusses reasonable methods and methodologies for modeling and understanding the software acquisition process. It is a secondary issue to present concrete models and discuss them (examples for presenting concrete models in this dissertation can be found in section 3.2.2, chapter 8 and the process shown in figure 9.1). The concrete models serve mainly as "examples of use" for the respective methods. This emphasis on modeling methodologies bases on the awareness that

- a firm consensus about a fixed model and a "clean" scientific justification of both its structure and quantification is hardly possible;

- the concrete structure of a model is highly dependent on the specific application domain and the characteristics of the respective projects to be modeled. From a scientific point of view, however, common structures and methodologies are more interesting.

So, we do *not* care, for instance, about the real influence of pressure on a group of people working on the development of software. We assume that the modeler already has a hypothesis about that influence – if this hypothesis

---

improvements

bases on social sciences, psychology, or the modeler's own experiences is irrelevant in the context of this dissertation. We solely care about reasonable ways to model and simulate hypotheses about software acquisition.

1.4. Overview

As aforementioned, this dissertation treats the application and innovation of techniques to better understand software acquisition projects. This work comprises four parts, and each single part corresponds to the application and/or innovation of one specific technique. Part II and part III could be seen as the core parts of this work. All parts – part IV is an exception due to its simplicity – are designed similarly: the first chapter of each part introduces the preliminaries or the basics of the respective field of knowledge; the part's remaining chapters present the actual scientfic treatment.

Part I uses graphical process modeling. A model, which we call GARP, capturing all aspects of the software acquisition process is described. This model is designed to be a comprehensive knowledge resource about software acquisition; it is *not* executable but solely a sophisticated assembly of static information. In view of this dissertation, the model can also be regarded as a (very detailed and comprehensive) definition, what we actually understand by "software acquisition".

Part I forms the basis for part II, where we describe a novel process simulation technique. It allows to map the material presented in part I as directly as possible to an *interactive* simulation, i.e. a game-like simulation in which the user is directly involved. There are similar techniques described in literature seeking to build software process simulation games; in contrast to these, however, our approach is focused on process steps which form its primary building blocks. The process-oriented interactive simulation approach is generic: it abstracts the detailed description of the actual project dynamics. An established method for describing the dynamics of systems could be plugged in here. One such method is System Dynamics.

Part III uses System Dynamics to model and simulate the dynamics of software acquisition projects. System Dynamics has widely been used to simulate the dynamics of software *development* projects. But there are, to the author's knowledge, no publications dealing with the simulation of software acquisition projects through System Dynamics. Therefore, the material presented in part III is novel, both to the System Dynamics community, and to the software process simulation community.

Part IV presents an approach to integrate System Dynamics in general and the System Dynamics model described in part III into the interactive simulation technique described in part II. Part V finally concludes this dissertation.

Figure 1.4, a classification tree, puts the contents of this work in the context of related research, and it additionally shows how part I, part II, part III, and part IV are interrelated. The solid arrows denote the subdivision of

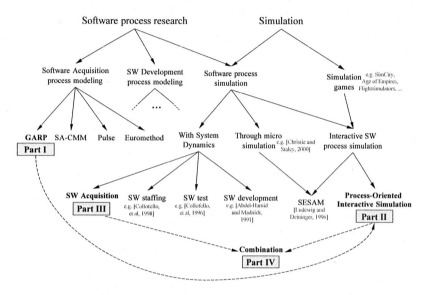

Figure 1.4.: Overview and classification of the research carried out in this dissertation.

research areas, and the dashed arrows denote dependencies among the parts of this dissertation. There are references put in gray font associated with some vertices in the tree; they denote example publications dealing with the respective research area. Figure 1.4 shows that the research carried out in this dissertation ranges between

- Process Modeling,

- Process Simulation with System Dynamics, and

- Interactive Process Simulation.

1.5. Contributions

This text is elaborate and in order to be self-contained, things are comprehensively introduced. For this, not every section contains novel scientific material. But the following issues can be seen as the actual contributions for the respective scientific communities:

1. The design of the generic software acquisition process model GARP (cf. section 3.2).

2. A framework for process-centered interactive simulation (cf. section 5.4).

3. A system theoretic view on the causes for acquisition's complexity (cf. section 1.2 (longer version) and section 7.4.2 (shorter version)).

4. A deductive design methodology for system dynamics models (cf. section 7.3).

5. A deductively designed framework for System Dynamics models for software acquisition projects (cf. section 7.4).

6. A complete system dynamics model of a software acquisition project (cf. section 8.3 and section 8.5).

7. An approach for combining System Dynamics and the process-centered interactive simulation approach (cf. section 9.2).

See chapter 10 for a more detailed treatment of the contributions of this dissertation.

1. Introduction

Part I.

Process Modeling

This part forms the basis for the rest of this dissertation, specially for part II; besides its actual contributions, it could also be seen as an extended definition explaining what we understand by "software acquisition". This part is actually about the design of a model of the software acquisition process, and about the integration of process knowledge from different sources, which represent facts in different degrees of abstraction, in a coherent model.

The research described in this part has its roots in a real-world project: a research and consulting department (at DaimlerChrysler research in Ulm), which has as one task the evaluation, customization, and implementation of methods and techniques for buying custom-made software, had the demand of a tool supporting the effective consulting of software acquisition projects. The tool should be a repository for knowledge needed to consult acquisition projects. Since this department works process-oriented, it seems reasonable that the respective tool should be a process model, or at least a process-model-like knowledge repository. There were several properties that the tool was required to have:

- The tool should be comprehensive enough to cover a great spectrum of project types (since at DaimlerChrysler, there exist many different kinds of software acquisition projects).

- The tool should be detailed enough to provide valuable practical information enabling a consultant to give concrete advice.

- The respective process steps should be temporally ordered.

The result of this process modeling effort, which includes the collection of a vast amount of knowledge about software acquisition projects and the subtle organization of this information, is a valuable contribution for the community: a process model which is comprehensive enough to cover a great spectrum of project types, which is detailed enough to provide practical information, and which temporally orders the process steps, is hard to build.

Chapter 2 sets the preliminaries about process models in common, and chapter 3 describes the process model, called GARP, representing the acquisition process both comprehensively and in great detail.

Chapter 2

Software Process Modeling

It has been recognized in the past, especially by software acquirers, that, where software plays a major role, process issues (i.e. issues concerning the way an organization or project works to achieve a certain goal) can have an important effect on the ability of software suppliers to deliver in time and in budget. In consequence thereof, there is a great interest in techniques to model and support software processes.

Since the 1960's, many descriptions of the classic software life cycle have appeared [6, 70, 74]. Royce [70] originated the formulation of the software life cycle using the now familiar "waterfall" chart.

This chapter gives a short introduction and overview on the issue of software processes and software process modeling. Section 2.1 defines what we understand by the term "process". A short common introduction to software process modeling is presented in section 2.2, and section 2.3 finally addresses possible purposes of software process models.

2.1. Software Processes

We provide two definitions of the term (software) "process". Definition 2.1 is due to the respective IEEE standard:

Definition 2.1 (Process.) *A sequence of steps performed for a given purpose; for example, the software development process.*

And definition 2.2 is due to Sommerville's textbook [82]:

Definition 2.2 (Software Process.) *The set of activities and associated results which produce a software product.*

As software systems are hard to build, complex, and purely immaterial, software processes are even more complex than other business processes, and they usually involve a large number of activities.

Interestingly enough, the attributes which can be assigned to software processes are similar to the attributes which can be assigned to software products. Some of these software process attributes are:

- *Understandability*: How detailed is the process described, and how easy is it to understand the process description?

- *Visibility*: Do the process activities culminate into clear results so that the progress of the process is easily visible?

- *Reliability*: Can process errors easily be avoided (or trapped) before they result in product errors?

- *Robustness*: Can the process be continued in spite of unexpected problems?

- *Maintainability*: Can the process easily be adapted to changing organizational requirements?

In close relationship to the issue of software processes is – according to the Software Engineering Body of Knowledge [78] – *software process engineering*. Software process engineering encompasses the definition, implementation, measurement, and improvement of the software engineering process.

2.2. What is a Software Process Model?

We provide a definition of "process model" in accordance with Ludewig [59]:

Definition 2.3 (Software Process Model.) *Description of a family of similar software development processes, or, in other words, a pattern structure of the organization and execution of software development processes.*

This definition assumes that a software process model describes – on an abstract level – a certain functioning type of software projects, and the model helps to classify the functioning of those projects.

Unfortunately, this is not the only possible definition used in literature. Some authors assign the term "software process model" a more common meaning, and they differentiate two types of software process models: first, there are *descriptive* models which seek to describe the functioning of one specific software project – possibly in all detail; process models of this kind describe one unique process, and they represent no template. Second, there are *prescriptive* or *normative* process models which come close to the above definition 2.3: prescriptive models define ways a project *should* be performed, and they define a certain type of software projects. Following this classification of software process models, the software acquisition process model GARP described in chapter 3 is prescriptive, whereas the system dynamics model described in chapter 8 is a descriptive model.

2.2.1. Elements of Process Models

Different elements of a process can be described and defined in definitions of process models, for instance activities, artifacts, and resources. There are, however, numerous formal and informal notations to describe processes – examples can be found in this dissertation in chapter 3 and section 5.4.1, or elsewhere in literature [80]. However, no standards or even de-facto standards for describing processes crystallized over the years. Therefore, we avoid to treat any specific modeling language here, but just state the elements which are commonly described in a process model, namely:

- *Activity*: Objective, entry and exit condition.

- *Process*: Set of activities.

- *Deliverable*: Tangible output of an activity.

- *Role*: Area of responsibility.

- *Communication*: Interchange of information between people or between roles.

- *Exception*: Description how to modify the process of some unexpected event occurs.

A process model may describe just a subset of these elements; the process model GARP, for instance, does neither specify roles, nor communication, nor any exceptions.

2.2.2. Types of Software Process Models

According to the "Software Engineering Body of Knowledge" [78], there are mainly two types of software process models, namely "Software Life Cycle Frameworks" and "Software Life Cycle Process Models":

- *Software Life Cycle Frameworks* are not detailed; they describe only high level activities and their respective interrelationships. Examples are the waterfall model, the evolutionary model, the spiral model, and the incremental software development model. The models treated in this dissertation, namely the GARP model, described in chapter 3, and the system dynamics model, described in chapter 7 and 8, are independent of the underlying Software Life Cycle Framework and they better fit the category of Software Life Cycle Process Models.

- *Software Life Cycle Process Models* are more detailed than Software Life Cycle Frameworks; often, Software Life Cycle Process Models do not attempt to order their processes in time. So, Software Life Cycle Process Models can be arranged to fit any of the Software Life Cycle Frameworks. Examples for Software Life Cycle Process Models are:

  - ISO/IEC 12207 and ISO/IEC 15504: These are standards prescribing the processes of software development and software acquisition projects; whereas they are more detailed than the descriptions of Software Life Cycle Frameworks, their descriptions are still on a quite abstract level.

  - The Capability Maturity Models: The Software Engineering Institute's CMM models are tools for benchmarking and improving software processes. Their process steps are not temporally ordered, but they are grouped in maturity levels which are evolutionary plateaus towards achieving a mature software process. Like the respective ISO standards, the CMM models are not detailed.

  - PULSE: This is a model of the software acquisition process, and it is, like the CMM models, meant as a tool for benchmarking and improvement of processes. Similar than in the CMM models, the process steps are not temporally ordered in PULSE.

  - GARP: This is a model of the software acquisition process developed in the scope of this dissertation. Its process steps are temporally ordered and, compared to the CMM model and the PULSE model, its process steps are detailed.

The fact that these examples are all Software Life Cycle Process Models, however, does not imply that these models all have similar purposes; some are standards, some are assessment models, and some are knowledge repositories.

But this classification is not the only possible way to discriminate process models. According to the different properties of process models and to the different ways that can be used to define and document a software process, there are further ways to classify process models:

- Process definition can be a policy, a procedure, or a standard.

- Process models can be generic vs. tailored, i.e. process models can be classified due to their level of abstraction.

- Process models can be descriptive vs. prescriptive vs. proscriptive.

Unfortunately, there is no data on the extent to which these different types of process models are actually used in practice.

2.3. Why Software Process Modeling?

In describing the purposes of process models, we adhere to the classification of process models in "Software Life Cycle Framework" and "Software Life Cycle Process Models" introduced in section 2.2.2.

Descriptions of Software Life Cycle Frameworks, for instance a waterfall model or a spiral model, are often employed during introductory presentations for people – for example for customers of custom-made software – who may be unfamiliar with the various technical problems and strategies that must be addressed when constructing large software systems.

The application of Software Life Cycle Process Models is more diversified. These models are defined for a number of reasons:

- Facilitating human understanding and communication: a defined process provides a means of reasoning about processes used to develop or acquire software, and it provides a basis for learning.

- Supporting process improvement: not until the process is clearly defined, project managers can specify where to improve the process and for what reason.

- Supporting process management: a defined process helps projects to run smoothly through providing a knowledge base of the project's functioning to all project members. Furthermore, a defined process protects against the dangers of ill-prepared crisis reactions.

- A defined process provides the basis for automated process guidance and automated process execution support.

The types of process definitions required will depend, at least partially, on that reason.

Chapter 3

GARP – A New Software Acquisition Process Model

This chapter deals with the design of a novel process model for software acquisition processes.

There are a few de-facto standard process frameworks [17, 64] which are well-established and commonly used to assess and improve software acquisition projects. Many things have been done and much effort has been spent on these models. They provide incitations and many helpful hints for our work. This chapter comprises many contributions for the process modeling community. However, this chapter neither presents a process model standing next to (or even in competition to) these standard frameworks, nor does it invent any novel process steps (which have been forgotten by all other acquisition process models), nor does it describe complete new ways to perform software acquisition projects. What we actually did is to build a tool supporting both acquisition project members and consultants (which are supporting acquisition projects) through

1. Collecting information about software acquisition.

2. Organizing this vast amount of information in a special way.

Our main requirements[1] for such a model are comprehensiveness, temporal ordered process steps, and sufficiently detailed descriptions of best practices

---

[1] Actually, these requirements stem from a project of a DaimlerChrysler research and consulting department. They actually serve the needs for a tool supporting the effective consulting of software acquisition projects; but these requirements and the tool "GARP" fulfilling these requirements are clearly applicable to many similar scenarios, for instance, training of project members or assessments of software acquisition projects.

for process implementation and process performance. Chapter 3.1 describes these requirements in detail and – since no current acquisition model satisfies these demands – derives the need to build a new software acquisition process model, which we call GARP for "**G**eneric Software **A**cquisition **R**eference **P**rocess". Section 3.2, the main part of this chapter, describes the design of the process model GARP by combining the strengths of existing approaches in a coherent way. GARP's use in improving software acquisition processes is presented in section 3.3, and section 3.4 eventually concludes this chapter.

3.1. The Need to Design a New Acquisition Process Model

The process model GARP should support process-centered consulting of software acquisition projects. In order to provide guidance to software acquisition project members, a process frame should be in place, where project members can single-out from a rough description certain aspects of the respective process; these aspects form the starting point to go into the details of process implementation or the improvement of existing processes. Since customers from a whole concern are consulted, the nature of the supported projects may therefore substantially differ. This requires extensive information resources both with regard to the process framework and the process implementation and improvement guidelines.

The following requirements for designing the process model result:

1. *Comprehensiveness.* The process model should include all relevant company specific aspects. Software acquisition projects performed at a huge international concern differ greatly among each other. The range goes from the procurement of world-wide e-business systems to embedded software in cars possibly already integrated in hardware units; and it goes from projects with many different suppliers, which again may have sub-suppliers to projects with one standard supplier. The process model should be applicable to all of them.

2. *Temporal Ordering of Process Steps.* An *explicit* guidance for software acquisition project members is required here. Ordered process steps can be used as a work sequence, which gives project members already a rough orientation.

3. *Sufficient Detailing.* Viewing things from a consultant's perspective, a main task is to give the acquisition project members advise on how exactly to do things better and provide them with specific hints and best practices for the respective process steps.

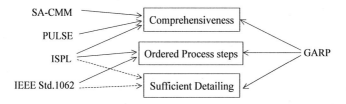

Figure 3.1.: Existing process models matching the GARP requirements.

The probably internationally most well-known process models for software acquisition, SA-CMM [79] and PULSE [64] – in fact they are comprehensive process frameworks – are clearly fulfilling the first requirement. They are designed to be sufficiently generic for use by any government or industry organization, regardless of size and acquiring products. In this respect, they are truly comprehensive. But since both models are designed for benchmarking and improvement and not for giving explicit guidance in performing acquisition projects, their process steps are not ordered. Furthermore, they both lack sufficient detailing. Though PULSE has some best practices associated with process steps (and capability levels), they are rather meant as indicators for process performance and not as advices on how to perform certain process steps. The structure of process steps in ISPL [44], a best practice library for the management of acquisition processes, has a work sequence character. Though the best practices are too high-level to be able to serve as an explicit guidance, ISPL is closest to the abovementioned requirements. Figure 3.1 shows some of the considered process models and the requirements, which we call "GARP requirements" in the rest of this chapter, they match.

To sum it up it can be said that, although there are currently many best practice guides and many acquisition process models in use, no one is both comprehensive enough to be used in many different projects and suitable as a ready to use cookbook for software acquisition (as far as this is possible – these issues are trade-offs). As all three requirements together are not fulfilled by any current model which is also indicated in figure 3.1, a model tailored to our needs is developed, which we call "GARP". The next section describes GARP's design principles and its structure.

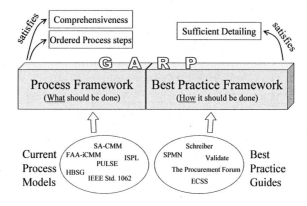

Figure 3.2.: An overview of GARP's architecture.

3.2. Building GARP

This section presents the development of the software acquisition process model fulfilling the above mentioned requirements by combining the strengths of existing approaches in a coherent way. Figure 3.2 gives an overview of GARP's design. It shows that GARP is made up of two parts: a process framework, which states *what* should be done in an acquisition project, and a best practice framework, where information is stored in a well structured manner on *how* to implement and perform process steps. The upper part of figure 3.2 shows that the process framework satisfies the "comprehensiveness" and the "ordered process steps" requirements and the best practice framework satisfies the "sufficient detailing" requirement. The lower part of figure 3.2 shows (some of) the information sources from which GARP was built.

3.2.1. Underlying Software Acquisition Process Models

Before starting to develop a software acquisition process model, we perform a survey [32, 33] to identify already existing software acquisition process models that might fit the needs. Some of the approaches which have a main influence on the model are described below:

- SA-CMM [79]: The Software Engineering Institute's "Software Acquisition Capability Maturity Model" follows the same architecture as the Capability Maturity Model for Software (SW-CMM), but with a unique emphasis on acquisition issues and the needs of individuals and groups who are planning and managing software acquisition efforts. In the SA-CMM an individual acquisition begins with the process of defining a system need. Some activities performed by the acquisition organization, such as planning, may pre-date the establishment of a project office. The SA-CMM includes certain pre-contract award activities, such as preparing the solicitation package, developing the initial set of requirements, and participating in source selection. In the SA-CMM, an individual software acquisition project ends when the contract for the products is concluded.

Since SA-CMM is a model for benchmarking and improving the software acquisition process, the process steps are not arranged in temporal or life-cycle aspects but in maturity levels – evolutionary plateaus towards achieving a mature software acquisition process.

- ISPL [44]: The predecessor is called "Euromethod". ISPL – in full, Information Services Procurement Library – is a best practice library for the management of software acquisition processes. A software acquisition process is the process of obtaining a system or a service or any combination thereof. The process steps and associated best practices are described in nine books:

  1. Introduction to ISPL
  2. Managing acquisition processes
  3. Specifying deliverables
  4. Managing risk and planning deliverables
  5. Dictionary
  6. ISP[2] in the european public sector: guidelines.
  7. ISP for web engineering
  8. ISP for large scale migrations
  9. ISP for IT service management

  ISPL covers a broad spectrum of project types and a temporal ordering of its process steps is presented. Unfortunately, the best practices are treated on a very abstract level. For instance, a best practice says that it is valuable to spend much effort on the request for proposal. But it does not say *how* to prepare the request for proposal.

---

[2]ISP is an abbreviation for "Information Services Procurement"

- PULSE [64]: A methodology[3] for assessment of software acquisition activities. It has similar goals as the SA-CMM. PULSE has been developed under the EC-SPRITE-S2 program. The project seeks to improve the acquisition processes (including procurement as a subset) of organizations involved in the acquisition of software products. The project combines two approaches to assist such organizations:

  1. first, by defining and verifying a formal methodology for identifying and assessing the processes used by such organizations for ICT[4] acquisition

  2. second, by identifying a set of organizational actions that improve the ways in which software acquisition projects are managed and that improve the measurement of the success of the ICT acquisition team

  The PULSE methodology consists of an acquisition reference model for processes, a process capability and a software acquisition assessment model, an assessment method, and an assessment tool.

  PULSE contains a comprehensive process framework for software acquisition, that classifies the relevant subprocesses into four process categories: Acquisition (ACQ), Support (SUP), Management (MAN) and Organization (ORG).

  As already mentioned, PULSE has some best practices associated with process steps. But these are rather meant as indicators for process performance and not as concrete advice on how to perform certain process steps.

- FAA-iCMM [24] In 1997, the Federal Aviation Administration (FAA) developed the FAA integrated Capability Maturity Model (iCMM) to guide improvement of its engineering, management, and acquisition processes in an integrated, effective, and efficient way. That model integrated three single-discipline CMMs that were being used separately in different FAA directorates: the Software Acquisition Capability Maturity Model SA-CMM, the Capability Maturity Model for Software SW-CMM, and a Systems Engineering Capability Maturity Model SE-CMM.

---

[3]In fact, PULSE is rather a "method" than a "methodology". A "methodology" is, as defined by the Merrian-Websters online dictionary, "a body of methods, rules, and postulates employed by a discipline". Nevertheless, we stick to the PULSE terminology and use the term "methodology" here.

[4]ICT is an abbreviation for "Information and Communication Technology"

- IEEE Std. 1062 [42]:

  The IEEE Std. 1062 describes a set of useful quality practices that can be selected and applied during one or more steps in a software acquisition process. It can be applied to software that runs on any computer system but is best suited for use on modified-off-the-shelf software and fully developed software. Since we mainly deal with acquisition projects for custom-made software products, it seems suitable as a basis for our process model. The standard contains the following sections:

  1. Introducing the software acquisition process

     - Software acquisition life cycle
     - Nine steps in acquiring quality software

  2. Software acquisition process

     - Planning organizational strategy
     - Implementing organizations process
     - Defining the software requirements
     - Identify potential suppliers
     - Preparing contract requirements
     - Evaluation proposals and selecting suppliers
     - Managing the supplier performance
     - Accepting the software
     - Using the software

3.2.2. The Process Framework

As mentioned in section 3.1, ISPL is the model, which is closest to the GARP requirements. An analysis of the way, software acquisition is currently done at DaimlerChrysler, merged with ISPL, formed the first version of the GARP model, and it is still its backbone. In order to make GARP comprehensive, we supplemented it with aspects from PULSE, SA-CMM, FAA-iCMM and IEEE Std. 1062.

Coverage

GARP's process steps cover the whole spectrum of acquisition activities: the GARP model starts with describing activities like defining the goals of the software acquisition, defining the technical requirements, project planning, tendering (which is GARP's most detailed part), driving the actual procurement process (which, for example, comprises process steps for joint risk management, joint reviews, and joint configuration management); the model ends with describing activities like acquisition acceptance, transitioning the acquired system to support and maintenance, and reviewing the completed project.

The process steps are hierarchically organized. GARP has four hierarchy levels, and the most detailed process steps are in the fourth hierarchy level. Since GARP contains a huge number of process steps – the tendering process step, for example, has 8 subprocess steps and more than 30 subsubprocess steps –, we will not show GARP's complete process framework. But in order to give an overview of its coverage the process steps of the first two hierarchy levels are listed below. There are only three process steps on the first hierarchy level, namely "Acquisition Initiation", "Driving the Procurement Process", and "Review Acquisition Project". They are printed in bold face. The process steps of the second hierarchy level, that is, the subprocess steps of the process steps of the first hierarchy level, are listed in italic shape under the corresponding process step of the first hierarchy level. Each process step name is accompanied by a short description clarifying its meaning.

Acquisition Initiation. Before choosing any suppliers, the acquisition has to be prepared and planned and the acquisition team has to be organized.

- *Acquisition Goal Definition*: The acquisition's target domain should be defined, and the actual goals of the acquisition should be clearly stated and the success criteria appropriately defined. Special financial requirements should be documented and the cost and benefits of the acquisition should be analyzed.

- *Tailor the Acquisition Project Process*: The company internal standard, a software acquisition reference process, should be scanned. The process steps which are not necessary should be eliminated and all process steps should be refined to an appropriate level of detail.

- *Refine Project Planning*: The project, quality, requirements, risk, and configuration management processes should be defined and a project, project organization, and quality plan should be specified. In parallel to this, all involved disciplines, for example the financial department, the departments responsible for legal aspects of contracts, and many more, should be coordinated and their special views and requirements should be taken into account, when defining management processes and specifying plans.

- *Develop Strategies for Transition to Support, Transition to Maintenance and System Implementation*: It is important to care as early as possible about support and maintenance strategies of the acquired system since this can have a tremendous effect on later strategic decisions.

- *Define Technical Requirements*: The requirements should be elicited, and negotiated with the stakeholders and interest groups. After that, they should be specified and documented and eventually validated and verified.

- *Acquisition Planning*: The acquisition's main risks should be analyzed and – based on insights gained through this (this is Euromethod's philosophy) – an acquisition strategy should be sketched regarding standards, types of suppliers (internal, external), types of tendering, the contract type, flexibility of contracts, potential suppliers, and many more aspects. "Acquisition Planning" also comprises determining the acquisition project's structure: identifying the various roles needed and allocating personnel to these roles.

- *Prepare System Integration*: An integration strategy should be developed for receipt, assembly, activation, and loading sequence that minimizes cost and assembly difficulties.

Driving the Procurement Process. As soon as the acquiring organization made clear the goals and the rough project plan, and fixed its internal structure, the actual procurement starts.

- *Tendering*: The request for proposal should be prepared (since experience shows that many acquisition project members require information about the request for proposal preparation, this is GARP's most detailed part). This comprehends, for instance, including the cooperation and communication requirements, the organizational constraints and procedures, the financial constraints, the legal clauses of the contract, the supplier evaluation approach, and many more activities. The request for proposal should be verified, released, and finally issued. A supplier should be selected according to the predefined selection strategy, and finally the actual contract should be prepared.

- *Procurement Monitoring and Controlling*: This is an important phase in the acquisition project. Shortfalls in the execution of this process steps can cause heavy losses in the project's benefit. The acquirer should conduct common risk, quality, configuration, requirements, problem, and contract change management with the supplier(s). Communication should work smoothly.

- *Acquisition Acceptance*: The receipt of each system element should be verified and the system element interfaces should be checked. A final validation of all procurement deliverables should be conducted.

- *Contract Completion*: The contract status should be reported and the contract should be closed regarding requirements, payments, and confidential information. Final decisions about contract completion should be performed.

- *System Integration*: The aggregates of system elements should be assembled according to the integration strategy and the assembled aggregates, and the complete system should be tested.

- *System Transition*: The actual system should be implemented and brought to operation. After performing operational tests, the system should be used (maybe in parallel with the old system). The users should be appropriately trained. Operational problems should be solved, and temporary work-arounds should be documented. User requests should be handled. The system's capacity should be monitored. If the new system works smoothly, the previous system can be retired. Eventually, the system should be transferred to support and to maintenance, according to the predefined strategies.

Review Acquisition Project. The suppliers, the performance of acquisition processes, and the performance of the management processes should be reviewed. Finally, the experiences made in the acquisition project should be described and possibly prepared for a software experience center.

We incorporated the whole spectrum of management processes in GARP, although a model with temporal ordered process steps is not fully capable of expressing their continuous dynamics. Basically, we integrated the management processes into GARP by splitting them into a planning process in the initiation phase and a corresponding process performing the management activities in GARP's "Driving the Procurement" part. For example, quality management is represented in GARP through the "Define Quality Management Process" and "Define Project Quality Plan" processes in the initiation phase and the "Quality Management" process in the "Driving the Procurement" phase.

Graphical Representation

GARP's process framework is based on a graphical representation. This allows straightforward use and fast navigation through the process steps. Figure 3.3 shows four sample pages of GARP showing the process steps of GARP's first and second hierarchy level, i.e. the process steps listed in the last subsection. Through these sample pages, we explain the structuring principles of GARP's graphical representation.

A process step is represented by an oval which is connected through arrows to other ovals. This forms the temporal ordering of process steps. For instance, the "Driving the Procurement Process"-page in figure 3.3 shows sequentially ordered process steps. If there is no reasonable temporal ordering between certain activities, process steps are be grouped concurrently in a dashed oval; the "acquisition initiation"-page in the left of figure 3.3 and the "review acquisition project"-page in the right of figure 3.3 show the concurrent ordering of process steps. Also shown in figure 3.3 is that hierarchy levels are connected through hyperlinks. If the user clicks, for instance, the oval named "Acquisition Initiation" – a process step of the top hierarchy level – then he is linked to the GARP-page shown in the left of figure 3.3. Some processes have an additional "?"-tag; these are hyperlinks to more detailed information about the respective process.

3.2.3. The Best Practice Framework

A model that says what should be done in what order is a useful tool in assessing running acquisition projects and in determining processes to be improved. But in order to provide the projects with suggestions on how to do it better, it is inevitable to get more concrete. We decided to enrich GARP with best practices from popular software acquisition guides. An overview on the most relevant guides is shown in figure 3.4.

In order to sketch the diversity of the different sources and the resulting difficulty of integrating them into GARP in a coherent manner, we give a short description of a few best practice guides:

- *Schreiber* [76]: This is a compact guide – only available in german, however – which gives orientation in procuring software. Schreiber's approach is document-oriented. For example, a specification document template is provided to guide the tendering process, and an evaluation document template is provided to guide the evaluation process. Schreiber's book is also very concrete and partly tailored to the swiss

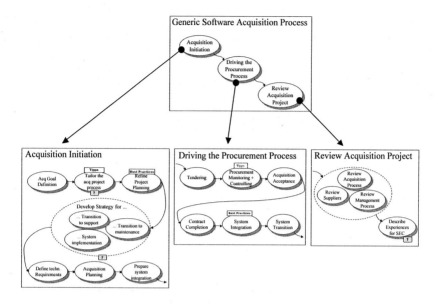

Figure 3.3.: Sample pages of GARP's process framework.

IT environment. Nevertheless, this book is useful specially for its concreteness.

- *The SPMN[5] Guide to Software Acquisition Best Practices* [81]: The guidebook's mission is, to help managers of large-scale software acquisition projects by identifying best management practices and lessons learned. In contrast to Schreiber's approach, this approach is activity oriented, and it is tailored to the US american IT environment and to the situation of huge defense projects.

- *The Procurement Forum* [63]: This is actually no concrete guidebook, but rather a forum for procuring companies to discuss and exchange experiences and for learning in improving acquisition projects and to solve procurement-related problems. The direct source of best practice information provided here is worth a lot. The best practices given through the procurement forum are often concrete, but, on the other hand, but sometimes only valid for very specific environments.

---

[5]SPMN is an abbreviation for "Software Program Managers Network"

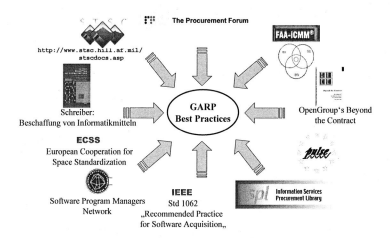

Figure 3.4.: Some of the sources used as best practice inputs for GARP.

- *IEEE Std. 1062* [42]: This standard – also used as an input for the process framework – describes a set of quality practices that can be selected and applied during one or more steps in a software acquisition process. The material presented in the IEEE Std. 1062 is very abstract and should be applicable to any IT environment.

- *ECSS* [21]: This is short for "European Cooperation for Space Standardization". It contains a set of standards which are intended for use in management, development, and quality control of space software projects. The best practices are tailored to huge projects and – in contrast to SPMN – to european projects. But the best practice information contained in the ECSS guide is still on an abstract level.

- *Validate* [56]: This is – like GARP – a collection of best practices from different sources. The authors studied procurements conducted by many organizations and analyzed the impact of applying certain best practices. Validate claims to show "which best practices really work and which are less efficient".

The graphical representation of GARP supports hyperlinks, and so it is obvious to link GARP's processes (typically those on the lowest process level) to a corresponding set of best practices. In doing this we face two main problems: the heterogeneity of the best practice sources, first in terms of the level of abstraction (e.g. ISPL provides quite abstract material whereas Schreiber gets very concrete) and, second, in terms of the kind of information provided (e.g. Schreiber gives document templates whereas SPMN is based on tips and hints).

Structuring Best Practice Sources

To keep GARP maintainable, all best practices should be traceable to their sources. In addition to linking each best practice information with its corresponding source we choose to structure the sources itself in order to cope with their diversity.

Thus we decide to record the following two criteria (see also figure 3.4) for each source in a subprocess's best practice collection:

1. *Level of coverage*: This criterion indicates how broadly the respective area is covered. Sources with a high degree of broadness could be used as a guideline to check if all important aspects of a subprocess are accounted for.

2. *Level of detail*: This criterion indicates the level of detail and the depth of treatment of the respective best practices. A high degree of detailing entails that best practices are directly implementable, whereas a low degree of detailing means that one has to instantiate and tailor the probably more abstract material.

Figure 3.5 is an extract of GARP showing the graphical representation of this structuring. The sources are points in a coordinate system; the x-axis represents the degree of broadness and the y-axis represents the degree of detailing of the respective information.

Structuring Best Practices

In order to deal with the above mentioned disparity in the kind of information provided by the best practice sources, we decided to organize the best practice material (of each GARP subprocess) into three information kinds:

1. *Document Template*: It consists of a proposal for the structure of the deliverable, usually in form of a table of contents, which should be developed in the context of the respective GARP subprocess.

2. *Detailed Procedure*: It provides a mini process describing the concrete implementation of the respective subprocess.

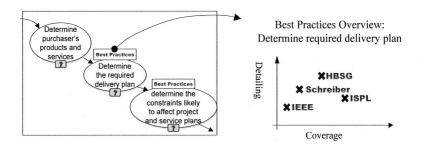

Figure 3.5.: Linkage of process steps to best practice sources.

3. *Tips, Hints and Dont's*: This is probably the most common form of best practice information. Suggestions are given what – based on experience – should be done or what should be avoided.

Managing the best practices' disparity in the level of abstraction turned out to be more difficult. We tried to deal with that by creating a "coherent view" of the best practices in each information kind category. This concretely means that, first, best practices from different sources in one information kind category should be kept free of redundancy, and, second, if specific information is available in different levels of abstraction, preference is given to those with the lowest level, i.e. those which are most easy to implement.

Overall Structure of the Best Practice Framework

In order to get the big picture of how best practice information is organized in GARP, figure 3.6 shows the structure of GARP's best practice framework. The numbered arrows denote hyperlinks from some text (or graphic) of one page to another page.

Clicking on the links in the best practice overview's coordinate system (arrow 1) leads to detailed information where exactly in the source the respective information can be found and to details about the source itself (arrow 3). Following the "coherent view"-link under the coordinate system (arrow 2) leads to an information-kinds list. From here, the best practices themselves can be accessed by following the "document template" (arrow 4), "tips, hints, and dont's" (arrow 5), or "detailed procedure" (arrow 6) links.

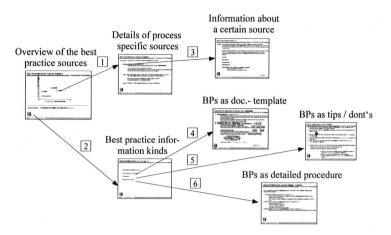

Figure 3.6.: The structure of GARP's best practice framework shown for one particular subprocess step.

3.3. Using GARP

Section 3.3.1 treats GARP's uses in software process assessments and improvements and section 3.3.2 deals with further applications of GARP.

3.3.1. Process Assessments and the Improvement Cycle

In a formal software process assessment, the process of a project or an organization is assessed against a *reference* process. The reference process is usually a standardized process framework like the SA-CMM, PULSE, or Euromethod. The assessment findings, which assign the project a rating – a capability or maturity level in the case of SA-CMM or PULSE – indicate where the project's process can be improved; these findings, however, usually do not indicate *how* to improve the process. GARP helps here, since it provides detailed information about the implementation, performance, and improvement of software acquisition processes. In fact, GARP is used both in performing software acquisition assessments, since it contains a comprehensive reference process, and in defining an improved software acquisition process. Figure 3.7 shows, how GARP supports this *improvement cycle* of assessing, improving, and installing processes.

So, GARP's process framework is used to define improvements in the

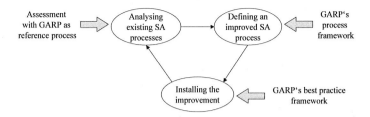

Figure 3.7.: GARP supports the software acquisition improvement cycle

assessed process (i.e. to define *what* to improve), and GARP's best practice framework gives suggestions, *how* to implement the improvements.

3.3.2. Further Applications of GARP

In addition to the use of GARP in the context of an acquisition process assessment as a source of best practices for achieving intended improvements, GARP proved valuable in other contexts, too.

GARP and Risk Management

GARP has been proven useful in performing risk management strategies and served as an impulse for novel ideas about risk management approaches in software acquisition projects.

GARP, influenced by ISPL, suggests to conduct an early risk analysis, even before the preparation of the request for proposal is conducted. The derived risk profile of the planned project is then used to fix the acquisition strategy (type and formality of monitoring activities, contractual aspects, density of milestones, and so on). This concept of an early and fast risk analysis for a planned project is further developed as a stand alone method [69], but of course the link to this concept still is part of the relevant subprocesses of GARP.

GARP as a Checklist for Existing Acquisition Concepts

GARP is well suited to review novel software acquisition concepts (in huge companies there are usually plenty of such "novel" concepts developed at the same time). One can use GARP's comprehensive process framework to test, if the concept comprises all relevant aspects; and GARP's best practice framework can be used to enrich the new concepts with additional information.

To give an example, at a specific passenger car development business unit at DaimlerChrysler, a concept for the management of software suppliers, called SLIM[6], was analyzed. The main areas covered in SLIM are monitoring software technologies and trends, scanning potential software suppliers, bidding, and contracting aspects. The analysis was conducted in the following way: for the topics covered in SLIM, it was checked, if related subprocesses in GARP and/or the best practices associated with these subprocesses could lead to an improvement of SLIM. According to GARP, the aspect of how the procurer and the supplier should cooperate during the project (e.g., common risk and problem management or common procedure when contractual aspects should be changed during the project) is not completely covered in the bidding procedure of SLIM. So the best practices in GARP related to the subprocess "Preparation of a request for proposal" has given helpful hints, how to enhance the SLIM concept in this aspect, especially as aspects related to requests for proposal, as a key document for acquisition, are treated very thoroughly in GARP.

GARP as Training and Guiding Material

The lifecycle orientation of GARP, its comprehensiveness, the association of best practices to the subprocesses, and the easy accessibility from the technical and the structural viewpoint convinced the management of a purchasing department of DaimlerChrysler in India to use GARP as a guide for the acquisition of software, especially as a guide for new members in their group. As a pilot application, one member of their group is introduced to GARP and this person has been successfully applied GARP's concepts in the running project.

3.4. Final Remarks

This chapter describes the need for a software acquisition process model tailored to the requirements "comprehensiveness", "sufficient detailing", and "temporal ordering of process steps". The construction process and structuring principles of such a process model are presented, and the use and usefulness of the model are shown.

---

[6]SLIM is an abbreviation for "Software Lieferanten Management"

Drawbacks of GARP

So far, GARP is a helpful tool for supporting specialists in consulting software acquisition projects and in process assessment and improvements. However, two things may prevent GARP from specially being suited as an educational tool: first, as our process model is very comprehensive novices get easily lost in details. Second, since it is a lifecycle model, it is neither fully capable of expressing the continuous dynamics of all the management processes, nor is it made for giving a grasp of how in detail the actual management of an acquisition process should work. Thus, in addition to further refining GARP itself, it is necessary to search for alternative representations of the information contained in GARP, if we want to make it more suitable for educational purposes – and this is definitely an aim of this work. The parts II, III, and IV deal with techniques allowing to impart knowledge about software acquisition projects more vividly.

Future Work – Not Followed up in this Dissertation

The ideas and the approach for the development of the process model could be valuable in other contexts, too, like software development processes or any kind of business process. It could be profitable to build similar knowledge repositories for other domains using the design principles described in this chapter.

Another option for future research (which is neither followed up in this dissertation) is a GARP based catalog of project situation patterns. Here, GARP's information is represented through a mapping of specific (patterns of) frequently recurring acquisition project constellations to a configuration of best practices which should be applied in the respective project constellation to achieve improvements. Clearly such a mapping only could be designed empirically after gaining a sufficient amount of experience with GARP.

3. GARP – A New Software Acquisition Process Model

Part II.

Interactive Simulation

The software acquisition process model GARP, presented in part I, is a well-proven tool for experts who support software acquisition projects. Due to its comprehensiveness, however, GARP is badly suited for novices, and it is definitely not suited for the illustration of problematic *behavior* in software acquisition projects; in fact, it is not capable of illustrating any kind of behavior. We seek to represent the information contained in the GARP model in a way that is more appropriate for the above-mentioned purposes. This part presents a method to represent GARP's information in an *interactive simulation*, that is, a simulation which allows a player to directly interact – a simulation game with the player taking the role of the project manager.

Chapter 4 presents the preliminary programming tools and techniques, namely functional and higher-order programming and some basics about the Scheme programming language, necessary for understanding the interactive simulation methodology and its implementation. Chapter 5 presents a novel interactive simulation methodology which treats process steps as first-class citizens; a process description, like the one presented in chapter 3, forms its basis. GARP, or any similar process description, is directly mappable to the presented interactive simulation framework.

Chapter 4

Excursus into Scheme and Functional Programming

The choice of programming techniques and the design of the interactive simulation framework are closely related. The implementation of the process interpreter described in section 5.4.4 is shaped through the underlying functional higher-order programming paradigm, and, in fact, the way it works is feasible only through the utilization of higher-order programming techniques. So, before presenting the actual interactive simulation technique in chapter 5, we present the needed programming basics in this chapter.

Section 4.1 introduces Scheme: its syntax, the most important data structures and functions, and DrScheme, a special programming environment for Scheme. Section 4.2 and section 4.3 approach the tools and techniques used to implement the interactive simulation from a more abstract and methodical point of view; these sections treat the programming paradigms, namely functional programming and higher-order programming, which are supported by Scheme, and which are the fundament of the design and implementation of the interactive simulation technique described in chapter 5.

4.1. Scheme and DrScheme

The interactive simulation technique described in chapter 5 is implemented in the programming language Scheme. This section introduces solely the (quite small) part of Scheme which is used to describe and which is needed to understand the implementation of the interactive simulation. It is far from being a comprehensive treatment of the Scheme programming language; for a self-contained and more systematic introduction to the Scheme programming language, the interested reader is referred to the respective literature [20, 26, 46].

Scheme is a statically scoped and properly tail-recursive dialect of the Lisp programming language. It has its actual roots in the λ-calculus [4]. Scheme has a clear and simple semantics and is widely used for teaching computer science [2]. Scheme's core language is small and simple. Nevertheless, it is easily extensible and supports a wide variety of programming paradigms including imperative, object-oriented, functional, and – most important for our purposes – higher-order programming styles. In higher-order programming, functions are first class values which allows to connect program components in flexible and elegant ways. This is a crucial feature for the implementation of the process interpreter: the basic requirement in the design of the process interpreter – as discussed in the next chapter in detail – is to allow dealing with process steps as "first-class citizens"; this, again, is accompanied by the requirement for the underlying programming language to support functions as "first-class citizens" which simply means that a language supporting higher-order programming has to be used.

4.1.1. Basic Syntax

In this subsection, we describe the basic Scheme syntax, namely the syntax of procedure evaluations and quotations which inhibit evaluations.

Evaluation

Scheme employs fully parenthesized prefix notation for programs and (other) data, even for common arithmetic operations. Any procedure application, whether the procedure takes zero, one, or more arguments, is written as

$$(\textit{procedure arg } \ldots) \quad \overset{\textit{yields}}{\Longrightarrow} \quad \text{The result of applying } \textit{procedure} \text{ to } \textit{arg} \ldots$$

Examples are:

$$(\texttt{+ 1/2 1/2}) \quad \overset{\textit{yields}}{\Longrightarrow} \quad 1$$
$$(\texttt{* 1/2 3}) \quad \overset{\textit{yields}}{\Longrightarrow} \quad 3/2$$

Procedure applications may be nested, e.g.

$$\text{(* (+ 1 1) (+ 1 2))} \quad \overset{yields}{\Longrightarrow} \quad 6$$

Not only procedure applications, but all structured forms and all lists are enclosed between parentheses.

Quotation

Through quotation, evaluation can be inhibited:

$$\text{(quote } obj) \quad \overset{yields}{\Longrightarrow} \quad obj$$

The quoted object is not evaluated; this allows *obj* to be employed as data. (quote *obj*) can be abbreviated with '*obj*. Examples are

$$\text{'a} \quad \overset{yields}{\Longrightarrow} \quad \text{a}$$
$$\text{'(+ 1 2)} \quad \overset{yields}{\Longrightarrow} \quad \text{(+ 1 2)}$$

Numerical constants, string constants, character constants, and boolean constants always evaluate to themselves; they need not be quoted.

Similar to (quote *obj*) is (quasiquote *obj*), which can be abbreviated with '*obj*. It allows parts of its text to be unquoted via (unquote *obj*), which can be abbreviated with ,*obj*. In a quasiquoted expression, nothing is evaluated except for the unquoted part. An example is

$$\text{`(1 2 ,(+ 1 2))} \quad \overset{yields}{\Longrightarrow} \quad \text{(1 2 3)}$$

The implementation of the interactive simulation uses quasiquotes and unquotes to generate tuples representing process steps; in such a tuple, the actual process step function is unquoted so that the function itself is part of the tuple.

4.1.2. Variable Bindings

This is not an exhaustive treatment of Scheme's binding constructs; we treat the most fundamental ones which are also used in the program code presented in chapter 5.

Variable Definitions

$$\text{(define } var \; exp) \quad \overset{yields}{\Longrightarrow} \quad \text{unspecified}$$

The command **define** creates a new binding of *var* to the value of *exp*.

Lambda Expressions

An important binding construct is the lambda expression:

$$(\text{lambda } formals \; exp_1 \; exp_2) \stackrel{yields}{\Longrightarrow} \text{ a function}$$

A lambda expression yields a function – a first class value in Scheme. In the next chapter, we will see that process steps are represented through lambda expressions, i.e. through functions. The formal parameters defined by *formals* of the function are bound to the actual parameters as follows:

- If *formals* is a proper list, then each actual parameter is bound to the corresponding element of the list. In this case, it is an error to provide too many or too few actual parameters to the function.

- If *formals* is an improper list, e.g. (x y . z), each variable but the last is bound to the corresponding actual parameter, and the last parameter is bound to the list of the remaining actual parameters.

- If *formal* is a single variable, then it is bound to the list of actual parameters.

Examples are:

$$(\text{lambda (x) (+ x 2)}) \stackrel{yields}{\Longrightarrow} \text{function}$$
$$((\text{lambda (x) (+ x 2)}) \; 10) \stackrel{yields}{\Longrightarrow} 12$$
$$((\text{lambda x (cdr x)}) \; 11 \; 22 \; 33) \stackrel{yields}{\Longrightarrow} (22 \; 33)$$
$$((\text{lambda (x . y) (car y)}) \; \text{"hello" "world"}) \stackrel{yields}{\Longrightarrow} \text{"world"}$$

Let Expressions

let establishes local variable bindings.

$$(\text{let } ((var \; val) \; \dots) \; exp_1 \; exp_2 \; \dots) \stackrel{yields}{\Longrightarrow} \text{ the value of the last expression}$$

A simple example is

$$(\text{let } ((x \; 1) \; (y \; 2)) \; (+ \; x \; y)) \stackrel{yields}{\Longrightarrow} 3$$

`let*` is similar to `let`

$$(\texttt{let*} \ ((\textit{var val}) \ \ldots) \ \ \textit{exp}_1 \ \textit{exp}_2 \ \ldots) \ \ \overset{yields}{\Longrightarrow} \quad \text{the value of the last expression}$$

but the values *val* are evaluated from left to right and each *val* is in the scope of the variables to its left, i.e. a value val_x can use a variable var_y provided that var_y occurs left of val_x.

4.1.3. Data Types

The implementation of the process interpreter uses lists, symbols and structs extensively; for the sake of completeness, we also mention Scheme's representation of numbers and booleans.

Except the structs, all data types mentioned in this section are part of the de-facto Scheme standard [46]. The MzScheme [26] extension of Scheme – a language also supported by DrScheme – provides possibilities in programming with structs.

Booleans

True and false are written as `#t` and `#f`. In conditional expressions, like `if`-expressions or `cond`-expressions, only `#f` counts as false; any other value counts as true, like, for instance, `#t`, lists, numbers, strings, and symbols.

Numbers

Scheme numbers are arranged in a tower of subtypes: integer, rational, real, and complex numbers. This classification is hierarchical: each integer is a rational, each rational is real, each real is a complex, and each complex number is a number. These types are defined by the predicates `number?`, `complex?`, `real?`, `rational?`, and `integer?`.

Lists and Pairs

In Scheme, a pair is built through the constructor procedure `cons`:

$$(\texttt{cons} \ \textit{obj}_1 \ \textit{obj}_2) \ \ \overset{yields}{\Longrightarrow} \quad \text{a new pair, whose \texttt{car} is } \textit{obj}_1 \text{ and whose \texttt{cdr} is } \textit{obj}_2.$$

Its most common use is to build lists, the most fundamental Scheme data structure. Lists are ordered sequences of pairs linked one to the next by the cdr field. The elements of a list occupy the var field of each pair. The cdr of the last pair of a *proper* list has to be the empty list, (). The cdr of the last pair of an *improper* list can be anything, but ().

Proper lists are printed as sequences of objects separated by white space and enclosed in parentheses and improper lists are printed in the *dotted pair notation*

$$(a_1 \cdots a_n \ . \ a_{n+1})$$

The values a_1 to a_n are the car parts of the respective pairs and the value a_{n+1} is the cdr part of the last pair. Examples for list and pair representation and printing are:

$$(\text{cons 1 (cons 2 (cons 3 ()))}) \overset{is\ printed\ as}{\Longrightarrow} (1\ 2\ 3)$$
$$(\text{cons () ()}) \overset{is\ printed\ as}{\Longrightarrow} (())$$
$$(\text{cons 1 (cons 2 3)}) \overset{is\ printed\ as}{\Longrightarrow} (1\ 2\ .\ 3)$$
$$(\text{cons 1 (cons (cons 2 3) ())}) \overset{is\ printed\ as}{\Longrightarrow} (1\ (2\ .\ 3))$$

The programmer has access on the two components of the cons-cell via the two selector functions car and cdr

$$(\text{car } pair) \overset{yields}{\Longrightarrow} \text{the first component of } pair$$
$$(\text{cdr } pair) \overset{yields}{\Longrightarrow} \text{the second component of } pair$$

The procedures caar, caddr, ... cdddar, and cddddr are compositions of the selector functions car and cdr. The a's and d's between the c and the r represent the application of car and cdr, respectively. Examples are:

$$(\text{cdddr '(w x y z)}) \overset{yields}{\Longrightarrow} (z)$$
$$(\text{caaar '(((x))))}) \overset{yields}{\Longrightarrow} x$$
$$(\text{caadar '((x (y)) z)}) \overset{yields}{\Longrightarrow} y$$

Strings and Symbols

A string is written as a sequence of characters enclosed in double quotes, for instance "This is a string".

Symbols are used for many purposes as symbolic names in Scheme programs. In most situations, strings could be used in the same way, but there is an important difference: comparison between symbols is much more efficient. Symbols can be converted in strings through the procedure `symbol->string`, and strings can be converted in symbols through the procedure `string->symbol`.

Structs

The implementation of the process interpreter uses structs to represent simulated objects in acquisition projects. Objects are for instance a supplier, a request for proposal, a project plan, and an error list.

A *structure type* is a record data type composing a number of fields. A *structure*, an instance of a structure type, is a first-class value that contains a value for each field of the structure type. The definition of a structure type has the following form:

$$(\texttt{define-struct}\ \textit{typename}\ (\textit{field}\ \ldots)\ \overset{yields}{\Longrightarrow}\ \text{a new structure type with name}\ \textit{typename}$$

A `define-struct` expression with n fields (automatically) defines a bunch of other names, among the most important are:

- `make-`*typename*: The constructor procedure; it takes n values corresponding to the respective n fields and yields an new structure of type *typename*.

- *typename*`?`: a predicate which returns `#t` if its argument is constructed with make-*typename*.

- *typename*-*field*: for each *field*, an accessor procedure which takes a structure value of type *typename* and extracts the value for *field*.

This is an example for defining a structure type and a corresponding structure and accessing a field in the structure:

```
(define-struct three-tuple (first second third))
(define a-tuple (make-three-tuple 'a 'b 'c))
```

$$(\texttt{three-tuple-second a-tuple})\ \overset{yields}{\Longrightarrow}\ \texttt{b}$$

4.1.4. Functions

Clearly, we cannot list all functions described in the Scheme "standard" (the "Revised[5] Report on the Algorithmic Language Scheme" [46]) and the numerous libraries provided by DrScheme. We confine ourself to describing the functions used by the implementation of the process interpreter described in the next chapter.

map

Map[1] is an important and powerful function in many functional languages.

$$(\texttt{map } procedure \; list_1 \; list_2 \; ...) \quad \overset{yields}{\Longrightarrow} \quad \text{list of results}$$

The number of formal parameters of *procedure* must equal the number of lists provided. Map applies *procedure* to corresponding elements of $list_1$, $list_2$, ... and returns the resulting list. Examples are

$$(\texttt{map } * \; \texttt{'(1 2 3) '(4 5 6))} \quad \overset{yields}{\Longrightarrow} \quad \texttt{(4 10 18)}$$
$$(\texttt{map (lambda (x) (+ x 2)) '(1 2 3))} \quad \overset{yields}{\Longrightarrow} \quad \texttt{(3 4 5)}$$

More detailed examples can be found section 4.3.1, where `map` serves as an example for higher-order programming concepts.

for-each

Similar to `map` is `for-each`

$$(\texttt{for-each } procedure \; list_1 \; list_2) \quad \overset{yields}{\Longrightarrow} \quad \text{unspecified} \quad ,$$

which applies *procedure* to corresponding elements of $list_1$, $list_2$, ..., but, in contrast to `map`, no list is returned; the results of the procedure are unimportant in this case. `For-each` is solely applied for the sake of the side-effects caused by the respective calls of *procedure*.

---

[1] For users of the functional programming language Haskell, it is interesting to note that Scheme's `map` is more general than the `map` function defined in the Haskell standard prelude. Scheme is dynamically typed in contrast to Haskell which is statically typed. A consequence is that, whereas Haskell program code may be easier to comprehend for novices, Scheme is more expressible than Haskell and particularly the *map* function can be (and actually is) defined more generally than in Haskell.

Similar things apply to `memq` and `and-list`.

assq

`Assq` uses association lists, i.e. proper lists whose elements must be pairs of keys associated with their corresponding value in the form (`key . value`).

(`assq` *obj assoclist*) $\overset{yields}{\Longrightarrow}$ the first element of *assoclist* whose `car` is *obj*, or `#f` otherwise.

The argument *assoclist* must be an association list. The procedure `assq` traverses the association list and compares the `car` part of each entry pair with *obj*. It returns the first entry pair whose `car` is equal to *obj*. It returns `#f` if no such pair exists. Examples are

(`assq 3 '((1 . "a") (2 . "b") (3 . "c")))` $\overset{yields}{\Longrightarrow}$ (3 . "c")

(`assq 3 '((1 . "a") (2 . "b")))` $\overset{yields}{\Longrightarrow}$ #f

apply

The implementation of the process interpreter's core (cf. section 5.4.4) uses the function `apply`.

(`apply` *procedure obj ... list*) $\overset{yields}{\Longrightarrow}$ the result of applying *procedure* to *obj* ... and the elements of *list*.

`Apply` invokes *procedure* with its first argument as the first *obj*, its second argument as the second *obj*, and so on. The elements of *list* are finally passed from left to right as the remaining arguments. Examples are

(`apply + 1 2 '(3 4))` $\overset{yields}{\Longrightarrow}$ 10

(`apply min 10 4 '(9 8 7))` $\overset{yields}{\Longrightarrow}$ 4

`Apply` is useful, when some or all of the arguments are provided in a list. It frees the programmer to destruct the list.

4.1.5. DrScheme

DrScheme [25] is a programming environment for Scheme. One of its strengths is the elaborate GUI framework portable between X Windows,

Microsoft Windows, and MacOS. This is, in fact, a crucial feature for our purposes and an important factor for choosing DrScheme, since other higher-order functional languages like Haskell [38] or ML [55] do not have such elaborate GUI building capabilities; though there are excellent ideas in the Haskell community about GUI design in purely functional languages [18, 73] the respective concepts are only prototypically implemented and hardly maintained and, up to now, not part of the Haskell standard.

DrScheme's Languages

DrScheme supports the R^{5}RS [46] Scheme programming language. It additionally supports a set of simpler sub-languages specifically designed for teaching students, and it supports a variety of extensions of R^{5}RS Scheme; crucial for our purposes are the following two extensions:

- MzScheme [26]: extends the R^{5}RS Scheme – amongst many other things – with structures and objects.

- MrEd [27]: extends MzScheme with a graphical toolbox for creating GUI applications (with special support for editor applications, hence the "Ed" in "MrEd").

MrEd provides the basic building blocks to create GUIs through a bunch of built-in classes such as `frame%`, `menu%`, `menu-bar%`, `menu-item%`, and many more. We finally provide an example of using MrEd's GUI utilities. A new frame can be defined by instantiating the `frame%` class:

```
(define a-frame (instantiate frame% ("A frame")))
```

A method *meth* of an object *obj* is called through

$$(\textbf{send } obj \ meth \ arg \ \dots) \quad \stackrel{yields}{\Longrightarrow} \quad \text{the result of applying } arg\dots \text{ to the } obj\text{'s method } meth.$$

We can open the frame shown in figure 4.1 by calling its `show` method.

```
(send a-frame show #t)
```

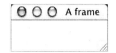

Figure 4.1.: A simple frame.

4.2. Functional Programming

The last section treated the technical side of the underlying tools to build the interactive simulation. We switch to a more abstract and high-level view here.

Functional programming is so called because a program consists mainly of functions. The functional programmer avoids the use of assignment and other side-effecting constructs. In *purely* functional languages like Haskell or Gofer, this is carried to an extreme: programs even consist *entirely* of functions having no side-effects.

The fact that a function call has no effects other than computing its result makes the order of execution irrelevant; when no side-effect can change the value of an expression, it can be evaluated at any time. The programmer needs not prescribe the flow of control, a task which is demanding and error-prone; his focus shifts from *how* to calculate a problem to *what* problem to calculate; in other words, the focus shifts to the specification of the problem. Altogether, we can claim that, compared to imperative programming, a more abstract, and thus more efficient, way of programming results from the functional style.

However, unlike other programming paradigms like object-oriented programming or aspect-oriented programming, which entail a gain in features, functional programming actually means avoidance or even loss of programming features like assignment and other side-effecting constructs. Languages supporting the functional paradigm must make up for this loss by providing powerful means for abstraction. Most common are automatic memory management, lazy evaluation, and – most relevant for our purposes – higher-order programming.

4.3. Higher-Order Programming

What makes functional languages like Scheme, Haskell, or ML specially suited for effective program development (specially the development of the process interpreter described in sections 5.4.3 and 5.4.4) is their support for *higher-order* programming including support for higher-order functions. Functions which themselves take functions as arguments and/or return functions as result are called *higher-order* functions.

Programming with higher-order functions is essential for the implementation of the process interpreter (cf. section 5.4.4). The requirement to have process steps as "first-class citizens" is accompanied by the requirement for the underlying programming language to support functions as "first-class citizens" which simply means that a language supporting higher-order programming has to be used.

Basic examples of higher-order functions (also used in the implementation of the process interpreter) and their applications are following.

4.3.1. Map

A prominent example is Scheme's built-in `map` function which is already described in section 4.1.4. A sophisticated use of the *map* function is the definition of a *subset*-function used in the implementation of the process-interpreter:

```
(define subset (lambda (xs ys)
                (and-list (map (lambda (x) (memq x ys)) xs))))
```

The expression `memq x ys` returns a true value if and only if the list `ys` contains the value `x`. The function `and-list` expects a list *bs* of boolean values and returns the conjunction of the values in *bs*.

The process interpreter's core algorithm is easily expressible via two nested applications of `map`.

4.3.2. Filter

The higher-order function `filter` has the form

$$(\texttt{filter}\ predicate\ list)$$

It gets *predicate* as its first argument and a list *list* as its second argument. It applies *predicate* to each element in *list* and returns a new list that is the same as *list*, but omitting all the elements for which *predicate* returned `#f`. An example is:

$$(\texttt{filter odd? '(1 2 3 4 5))} \xRightarrow{yields} \texttt{'(1 3 5)}$$

4.3.3. Compose

Not only functions but whole programs can be easily glued together through the higher-order function `compose`:

```
(define compose (lambda (f g)
                  (lambda (x)
                    (f (g x)))))
```

Compose is a function of two arguments `f` and `g` which have to be functions of one argument; its result is the composition $f \circ g$. An example for its use is:

```
(map (compose
       (lambda (x) (* x 10))
       car)
     '((1 2 3) (4 5 6) (7 8 9)))
```
$\overset{yields}{\Longrightarrow}$ (10 40 70)

4.3.4. Glue and Modularization

Even through these quite basic examples, one can see that higher-order functions provide a powerful form of function *glue* [40]. It is this glue which enables effective *modular* programming – in modular programming, one solves a problem in dividing it into subproblems and, after solving the subproblems, glues them together to the solution. So, the possibilities of glueing program parts together is directly related to the language's capabilities to modularize problems. Powerful modularization capabilities support abstraction, and programs get shorter and more elegant.

It is exactly this sophisticated form of function glue which forms the fundament for the implementation of the interactive simulation, specifically for the "process interpreter" (whose implementation is described in full detail in section 5.4). The process interpreter glues functions, representing process steps in an acquisition process, together and builds the actual simulation of an acquisition project out of them. Thus, the benefit we gain from this sophisticated forms of function glue is, that we are capable of encapsulating the program code pertaining to the implementation of a specific process step; this makes the program code maintainable: it is easy to add or remove process steps from the implementation.

4. Excursus into Scheme and Functional Programming

Chapter 5

Process-Oriented Interactive Simulation of Software Acquisition Projects

This chapter presents a new simulation technique which allows to map the information contained in GARP as directly as possible to such a simulation. This simulation technique is

- *interactive*: according to existing literature in game-like simulation of software processes [50, 75], we call simulations in the form of a game *interactive*. The player closely interacts with the simulation. A simulation run is neither monolithic nor predetermined, but highly dependent on the player's decisions.

- *process-oriented*: Unlike any other interactive simulation technique described in literature, an ordered set of process steps forms the basis in the design of this simulation technique. The high-level goal is that GARP and any similar process model should be mappable as directly as possible to an interactive simulation.

Chapter 5.1 points out in detail the importance of having a facility which explains the actual dynamics of an idealized acquisition project to novices. It discusses the question why an interactive simulation is a suitable facility for this. Chapter 5.2 positions the work presented in this chapter in relation to the current research landscape. In chapter 5.3, past research in interactive software process simulation is reviewed and compared to our special requirements for an interactive simulation system. What should be the scope of such an interactive simulation, and how should it basically be designed? Chapter 5.4, which could be seen as the central contribution of this chapter, tries to answer these questions. A process-oriented interactive simulation framework and its instantiation to a small part of GARP are presented. Chapter 5.5 describes techniques to embed best practice knowledge in the simulation framework, and chapter 5.7 gives concluding remarks and an outlook on possible future work.

5.1. Training and Understanding the Software Acquisition Process

The design of a process model (like GARP) should be followed by activities concerning its utilization. The following points seem to be particularly important in the context of utilization:

- Utilization mainly depends on management compliance. As extensive documentation is seldom read thoroughly by busy managers, we search for representations to make the process model both understandable and attractive to decision makers. We search for a sort of promotion.

- For a project to run smoothly, *every* staff member should have a clear grasp of how the project dynamics should ideally look like. Many problems in complex projects stem from a lack of transparency of the project's process and a lack of transparency on how this process should ideally be transferred into the every day work.

- Due to the growing number of complex software acquisition projects, there is an increasing need for well-trained and experienced project leaders. Thus, another major issue is education and training.

Three things prevent GARP from being specially suited for promoting and understanding. First, as the process model is comprehensive, novices get easily lost in details. Second, since the process steps obey a strict temporal ordering, GARP is neither fully capable of expressing the continuous nature of all the management processes, nor is it made for giving a grasp of how in detail the actual management of an acquisition project should work. Third, GARP is a static description of an acquisition process and not executable in any way. Therefore, it is not possible to illustrate any kind of behavior, specially problematic project behavior, with GARP. This is inevitable for education and training purposes, however.

Providing a slim copy of GARP is not the solution and just another document on the desks of managers and project members. Ludewig [49] has expressed the idea to develop a teaching game where computer science students can play the role of a software project manager, and this is – with a slightly different focus – an excellent means to tackle the above mentioned issues: the player of the simulation is able to learn facts about successful performance of acquisition projects and experience the behavior and dynamics of the project's course.

5.2. Positioning of this Approach

The tree shown in figure 5.1 shows how the research presented in this chapter can be classified in relation to the current research landscape. It shows

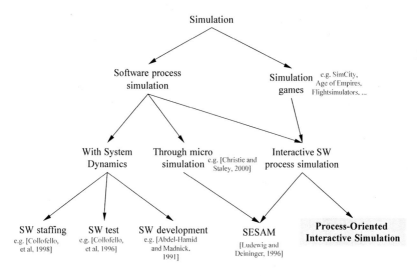

Figure 5.1.: Influences, dependencies, and correspondences to other simulation paradigms

different simulation paradigms and their influence on active research in software process simulation. Looking at the left branch of this tree, we see that basically three paradigms have been used to simulate software processes:

- *The system dynamics approach*: System Dynamics is probably the most widely used technique to simulate software processes. We use it in part III to build a model of the software acquisition process.

- *The microsimulation approach*: this is a bottom-up approach. Solely the small things are simulated, and the focus is on the emergent behavior. It has been used, for instance, in the simulation of the requirements process [13].

- *The interactive simulation approach*: there are very few research projects using this approach; an example is the SESAM project, which is sketched in section 5.3.4.

Also combinations of these paradigms are conceivable to examine software processes. An example is the combination of micro-simulation with interactive simulation as used in the SESAM approach. Another example is the combination of System Dynamics with interactive simulation as used in research performed in the context of this dissertation. This is described in section 9.

Looking at the right branch of the tree shown in figure 5.1, we see that interactive simulation is a technique to build games representing a certain domain. An example of a commercially successful simulation game is *SimCity* [77]. The player has to manage the development of a city, and his goal is to let the city flourish. He can introduce certain policies, build streets, railroads, or plots, and enable other possibilities for growth. Similarly, the player of an interactive software process simulation has to manage the course of a project, and his goal is to let the project flourish and to run it in time and on budget. He can introduce certain policies, manage and control the workforce, or summon project meetings and thus lay foundations for a smooth flow of the project. The process-oriented interactive simulation approach can be seen as a new branch in interactive software process simulation research and is positioned as a sibling of SESAM in figure 5.1.

5.3. Past Research in Interactive Simulation

In sections 5.3.1 to 5.3.4, we examine similar research projects, which are not necessarily part of the software process community. In terms of figure 5.1, we examine work located under the node "Interactive SW process simulation" but also work located under "System Dynamics" or "Simulation games" if they touch our issues.

The SESAM project presented in section 5.3.4 is probably the most relevant related work for our case. Section 5.3.5 presents the special needs on which the design of the process-oriented simulation framework is based.

5.3.1. Software Process Flight Simulation

With the pioneer work of Abdel-Hamid and Madnick [1], software process simulation through System Dynamics became popular. A technique called "Software process flight simulation" evolved. Such a "flight simulator" is basically an executable system dynamics model enhanced with a "cockpit", or interface, which contains the specific controls that reflect decision making in real projects. Software process flight simulators were used for prediction, for example for predicting the impact on productivity when moving an organization to the highest CMM maturity levels [72], and for education and training [53]. Although this simulation methodology provides insight into the impact of important decisions, the player can hardly feel to be involved in the project's process. System dynamics simulation is based on a static view of the software project; the respective models are executed in batch mode: when the scenario is defined, the *whole* project is simulated; a simulation run is monolithic. The player of a software process flight simulator can just handle some knobs and switches and finally watch the outcome of the project.

5.3.2. The CBT Training Module

A recent flight simulation approach to software process simulation with a higher player involvement is the computer based training (CBT) module [60] developed at the IESE and the University of Kaiserslautern. It is based on a system dynamics model (calibrated with the help of Boehm's COCOMO model) [7, 8]. A main feature of CBT's model is the player's ability to change parameters at any time during the simulation run and the possibility to apply for example code or design inspections – this is represented through special parameters in the system dynamics model.

5.3.3. The RENAISSANCE Project

Contrary to process flight simulation, the RENAISSANCE project [88] provides an approach for learning with a high degree of player involvement. The renaissance court of Urbino at around the 14th century is simulated through a multi-user role playing game over the Internet. Social life during renaissance was subject to plenty of subtle behavioral rules, and users of the RENAISSANCE game should be enabled to experience this life as realistically as possible. A player seeks to achieve the highest score among the involved players. The score is expressed in "fame", "fortune", "faith", and "force". A 3D-graphics rendering machine, local to each client, provides realistic impressions. An extra authoring tool allows domain experts with no knowledge in computer science and formal languages to describe and change the respective rules.

5.3.4. SESAM

"SESAM" is an abbreviation for "Software Engineering Simulation through Animated Models". Although SESAM's structure is quite different from the process-oriented interactive simulation approach presented in this chapter, we take a close look on its underlying principles and functioning; the reason is that SESAM is – as far as the author knows – the only simulation approach in the software process community enabling a high player involvement, and, thus, SESAM is the only approach described in literature pursuing goals which are similar to ours. Therefore, a comparison to our approach is of special interest.

SESAM is the result of a big research effort at the University of Stuttgart. The simulation system passed through several years of development. SESAM [50, 75] is an approach to develop quantitative dynamic models of software development projects. It comprises a corresponding notation and a simulation system. The notation's semantics can be exactly specified through attributed graph grammars. This makes it suitable of being automatically executed; in the case of SESAM, this execution results in a project simulation game. The basic requirement in designing SESAM was that *no* model should be hard-wired in the system. The aim was to design a tool that enables the modeler to easily build up and rebuild executable models of software development projects.

Due to the statements of SESAM's authors [50, 75], the modelers always are in the area of conflict between naive simplification of complex interrelations and unmanageable complex models, which cannot serve their actual purpose, namely the better understanding of software processes.

The Structure of SESAM Models

A dynamic SESAM model is made up of three parts:

- a SESAM *schema*
- a *situation model*
- rules

The part of reality to be modeled is conceived as a system of objects and their mutual relationships; this view is mapped to a system of entities and corresponding associations. Entities and associations are arranged in classes. A SESAM schema defines which classes and associations may appear in a model. In building a schema, one therefore determines the part of reality which will be simulated, or, in other words, one determines the system boundary. The Schema defines, so to speak, the micro-world of the simulation to be built.

But note that a certain schema does not specify a simulation model for a concrete project; it is rather a basis for simulation models for a whole class of projects. However, a certain instance of a schema – called *situation model* – is specific for a concrete situation in a concrete project. Figure 5.2 shows the relationship between classes, their instances, and a concrete SESAM model.

Figure 5.2.: Elements of SESAM models

Rules

A fundamental decision in designing SESAM was, not to connect the description of the project dynamics with the classes but with typical patterns of project scenarios. Applicability conditions for rules in SESAM are situation models with formal parameters. A rule is applied when a fitting part of the situation model, i.e. a partial graph which is homomorphic to the graph forming the applicability condition, is found. Generally, rules do not "fire"; they are rather activated for a certain period of time, namely as long as the corresponding graph pattern in the situation model persists; the respective model is thus called a *continuous effect model*. Additionally, rules can be defined representing sudden effects; they are deactivated directly after firing.

Bottom-line

The basic idea of SESAM is to build up an understanding of project dynamics in a bottom-up manner, that is, just "small" things are simulated, and there is *no* such thing like a process built into the simulation system. All effects and actions of a project are considered as the results of microscopic effects and atomic actions between the basic elements (like certain documents, the simulated employees, or the costumer) of the SESAM model. Thus, SESAM is a micro simulation – some may also call it *micro-analytic* simulation – approach. SESAM is interactive and "real-time": its basic elements are interacting the whole time while the user is playing. SESAM is based on a static model described in an entity-relationship-like manner and a dynamic model which is basically a large set of rules. The rules can express evolutionary changes of attribute values controlled by other attribute values – these are exactly the rules expressible in System Dynamics – and revolutionary changes, which effect the game state graph structure.

Although SESAM and the process-oriented interactive simulation approach presented in this chapter follow the same goal, namely designing game-like simulations of software processes for better understanding, they greatly differ. Table 5.1 sums up the main differences.

5.3.5. Our Special Needs

Like in SESAM, in an interactive simulation, as we want to understand it, everything but the project leader is simulated; the player of the simulation game takes its role. But both, the SESAM and the CBT module, are tailored to the needs for simulating software *development* processes, and neither of them is specially designed for simulating software acquisition.

Even more important, we need an interactive simulation methodology where a process step is *first class citizen*. This particularly means that a process description (like GARP), which expresses temporal ordering, concurrency and non-deterministic choice of process steps, should be mappable as directly as possible to an interactive simulation. We call this desired property *process-orientation*. Neither SESAM nor the CBT module is process-oriented; this makes it necessary to build a novel interactive simulation approach tailored to our needs.

The fact that a process should form the basis of the interactive simulation entails further requirements: a process is never fixed; it is growing and changing as our experiences with it are growing, and so the simulation's design has to ease addition and removal of program code representing process steps. This suggests that every process step should be encapsulated and demands a strong separation of the simulation's part containing the processes from a generative process engine – which we will also call *process interpreter* (cf. section 5.4.3 and 5.4.4) – that glues the processes together and builds the actual interactive simulation out of them.

Sesam	Process-Oriented Interactive Sim.
rule-driven	process-driven
Solely the small things are simulated.	A framework for expressing the simulation of "big" things, that is, the process steps and the overall process.
The project's course on the grand scale is expected to arise by itself. The principle of the formation of higher-order structure from the simulation of small things is called *emergence.*	How the project's course on the small scale can be described and implemented is left open. Though System Dynamics proves to be an appropriate method for filling this gap, the process-oriented method is not bound to a specific description method.
SESAM is concrete. A simulation run represents the view of a person which is fully involved in the project.	The process-oriented interactive simulation is more abstract. A simulation run represents the view of higher management on a project.
Example: simulating quality assurance	
Quality assurance is not an abstract factor in SESAM but it is represented through concrete activities like the establishment of coding standards or the preparation of review sessions. In order to ensure a tight quality assurance system, the player must continually initiate the respective activities in the daily project work.	Quality assurance may be represented solely through an abstract numerical factor, which influences the project course. However, the modeler has the liberty to model quality assurance as concrete as he wants with a technique of his choice.

Table 5.1.: Differences between SESAM and process-oriented interactive simulation.

5.4. A Process-Oriented Interactive Simulation Framework

This section is central to this chapter. It treats the question how a process-oriented interactive simulation could basically be designed. Section 5.4.1 serves as the basis: it introduces a description method for processes. This lays the foundations for the later sections. The brief section 5.4.2 explains the decision to model process steps as Scheme functions, and the sections 5.4.3 and 5.4.4 treat the design and functioning of the framework's core: the process interpreter.

5.4.1. Process Description for Interactive Simulation

It has been pointed out in the past that process descriptions with an overemphasis on the modeling of tasks could be counterproductive since this limits human flexibility and leads to complex models. An alternative are entity process models [41]; they are focused on real-world objects like requirements documents or test cases which persist throughout the complete process. Since it weakens complexity, we take a similar approach here which stresses the product-oriented aspect of software processes. Katayama's hierarchical and functional software process description method HFSP [45] proves to be useful in designing the simulation system: it is straightforward and due to its functional perspective near to a programming language. It emphasizes the importance of the product-oriented aspect of software processes which should be the first thing to deal with. Furthermore, HFSP is coherent with latest efforts to describe processes in executable languages (for instance programming languages) [10, 58]; in this respect, Osterweil claims that "Software Processes are Software, Too!" [57].

Figure 5.3 shows a (simplified) part of GARP's acquisition processes in an HFSP-like notation. For reasons of clarity, we provide a coarse and simple model of the software acquisition process here: the process says that software is procured ("procure-software" is the top-level process step) either through buying a COTS product or through a sequence of process steps, namely tendering (i.e. through preparing and issuing the request for proposal and selecting an appropriate supplier), contract preparation, supplier monitoring (which includes contract change management, quality control, and risk management), and, finally, acquisition acceptance. The reader can find a more detailed HFSP-description of the software acquisition process in section 9.1.

Katayama treats process steps, in the first approximation, as mathematical functions, denoted by

$$A(x_1, \ldots, x_n | y_1, \ldots, y_m),$$

---

types:
    concrete-supplier, contract, request-for-proposal,
    request-for-proposal-issued, sw-product

activities:
procure-software (| sw-product) $\Rightarrow$
    tendering (| concrete-supplier)
$\mathcal{P}$ prepare-contract (concrete-supplier |
                      concrete-supplier, contract, sw-product)
    monitor-supplier (concrete-supplier, contract, sw-product |
                      concrete-supplier, contract, sw-product)
$\mathcal{A}$ acquisition-acceptance (concrete-supplier, contract, sw-product |
                      sw-product)

procure-software (| sw-product) $\Rightarrow$
$\mathcal{P}$ buy-CoTS-product (| sw-product)

monitor-supplier (concrete-supplier, contract, sw-product |
                 concrete-supplier, contract, sw-product) $\Rightarrow$
$\mathcal{A}$ contract-change-mgmt (concrete-supplier, contract |
                      concrete-supplier, contract)
$\mathcal{P}$ quality-control (concrete-supplier, sw-product |
                      concrete-supplier, sw-product)
$\mathcal{P}$ risk-mgmt (concrete-supplier | concrete-supplier)

tendering (| concrete-supplier) $\Rightarrow$
$\mathcal{P}$ prepare-rfp (| request-for-proposal)
$\mathcal{P}$ issue-rfp (request-for-proposal | request-for-proposal-issued)
$\mathcal{A}$ select-supplier (request-for-proposal-issued | concrete-supplier)

Figure 5.3.: The procure-software process; a simplified part of GARP, in an extended HFSP notation.

from input objects $x_1, \ldots, x_n$ to output objects $y_1, \ldots, y_m$. The textual ordering of an activity's subactivities is *not* significant. Temporal ordering, concurrency, and non-determinacy are expressed implicitly through object dependencies. The "tendering"-activity shown in figure 5.3, for example, occurs prior to the "prepare-contract"-activity; the latter requires the "concrete supplier"-object, which the "tendering"-activity provides. The subactivities of the "monitor-supplier"-activity may be activated in unspecified order or concurrently since there are no input/output - dependencies between them. The process is non-determinate since there are two definitions of the "procure-software"-activity.

An extension to the HFSP notation is that atomic actions, that is, actions which are not further decomposable, are marked with either $\mathcal{A}$, for "active", or $\mathcal{P}$, for "passive". Passive actions can be activated solely by the player of the simulation. Active actions occur without the player's initiation – they can activate themselves, which is why they are called "active" – and are actually *reactions* to external events. The "select-supplier"-action, for example, is active since the player must react to incoming offers. The simulation system handles active actions in a slightly different way.

We conclude this subsection with a general remark about the meaning of HFSP descriptions. A line in the HFSP description of a process can be viewed under two different angles:

1. It can be viewed as a process step solely describing *what* to do, but not *how* to perform the respective process step. With respect to its level of abstraction, it is thus comparable to the process descriptions of GARP's process framework.

2. It can be viewed as a function name and its signature. It describes inputs and outputs of that function, but it does not say how the function actually works.

Since the HFSP notation allows both point of views, it provides a direct link from process modeling to programming languages; this is the reason why we treat the HFSP notation in such a detail here. As the following sections will show, a process description in extended HFSP is directly mappable to an interactive simulation.

5.4.2. Process Steps as Scheme Functions

We can benefit from many advantages of functional languages [40], if we encapsulate a process step in a function of the programming language.

Figure 5.4 shows an extract of the simulation system's process part. The

```
      ⋮
(define prepare-rfp
  (lambda ()
    (let ([rfp-quality (get-number "How much effort do you want
                                    to spend on the rfp
                                    (in person hours)?")])
      ...
      (make-rfp ... rfp-quality ...)))))


(define issue-rfp
  (lambda (request-for-proposal)
    ... (make-rfp-issued ...)))
      ⋮
```

Figure 5.4.: An extract of the simulation system's process part.

function `prepare-rfp` points out how activities can interact with the player: the function `get-number` opens a dialog, asks the player to enter the effort he wants to spend on the request for proposal and stores the provided value in `rfp-quality`. The function `prepare-rfp` adjusts global parameters, for instance, resources spent, money earned, and many more. This is, however, not shown in figure 5.4, since we do not focus on the actual design of the process step functions in detail but rather on mechanisms to combine these functions to an interactive simulation. In designing the actual function bodies, GARP's best practice framework proves to be useful. It provides guidelines to decide which parameters should to used and how they should be changed when a certain action is activated (we go into more detail in section 5.5). Eventually, the function `prepare-rfp` returns an `rfp`-object.

These process step functions form the main input for the process interpreter.

5.4.3. The Process Interpreter – Functioning

We call the program part responsible for building the simulation out of the list of process tuples the *process interpreter* due to the similarities to interpreters of program code. The interpreter works up the process step functions and compiles them into an interactive simulation. Figure 5.5 shows what the

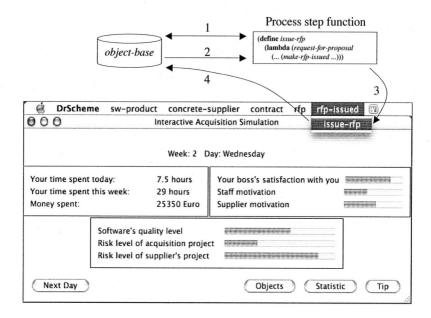

Figure 5.5.: The process interpreter's basic mode of operation

process interpreter is doing for one passive process step (the interpreter treats active process steps slightly different). But note that the look of the interactive simulation shown in figure 5.5 is just one example for the realization of the framework.

The `object-base` contains objects – for instance, a supplier, a contract, and a request for proposal – which are currently available to the player. First, the interpreter determines if the process step is *executable* by testing (arrow 1) if all input objects for the activity are available in the object base or, more formally, if the following condition holds

$$\forall i \in input_p : \exists o \in object\text{-}base : \textbf{type}(o) = i,$$

where p is the respective process step, and $input_p$ is the set of input objects of p. Only if this process step is executable, the interpreter creates a corresponding menu item. Finally, the interpreter connects the menu item with the actual function (arrow 3) with its parameters instantiated to the respective objects in the *object-base* (arrow 2). After each execution of a process step by the player, the object base is updated (arrow 4) and the process interpreter passes through all the functions which represent process steps and adapts the menus accordingly as shown in figure 5.5.

5.4.4. The Process Interpreter – Implementation

This subsection describes how the process interpreter uses higher-order programming concepts to elegantly update menus and menu items in the course of a simulation run.

Objects and Process Steps

We begin with describing the exact realization of the object and process step storage; this might seem not particularly interesting; it is, however, a preliminary to understand the process interpreter's core functions `executable-processes`, `create-menu-items`, and `instantiate-func`, which are treated at the end of this subsection.

There are two kinds of data underlying the process-oriented simulation: objects and the process step functions. Objects are the simulated real-world entities relevant for the simulated part of reality. Examples for objects in the simulation of a software acquisition project are a supplier, a request for proposal document, the staff, or a contract. Objects which are available to the player are stored in the variable `object-base`, which is initially the empty list. The following is an example value of the `object-base` after a few player actions in a simulation run:

```
((request-for-proposal rfp-v0.9 . #(struct:request-for-proposal))
(project-plan project-plan-v0.9 . #(struct:project-plan))
(staff initial-staff . #(struct:staff)))
```

The variable `object-base` is a list of three-tuples (cf. page 53 for a detailed explanation of the structure of n-tuples and lists). The first element of each tuple is a symbol representing the name of the respective object type, the second element is a symbol representing the name of the respective object and the third element is a struct containing the actual data of the object.

The value `process-base` stores all atomic process steps (i.e. process steps which are not further decomposable) with their respective information in a list of 5-tuples. A tuple's first value is a string used by the GUI, the second and third values are the lists of input and output objects respectively, the fourth value is the process step function itself (see figure 5.4 for example definitions of activity functions), and the last value tags the activity as "active" or "passive". The following shows the definition of the `process-base` (only two definitions of process step tuples are explicitly shown therein):

```
(define process-base
  (list
    ...
    (prepare-rfp (staff)
                 (request-for-proposal)
                 ,prepare-rfp pass)
    (select-supplier (request-for-proposal staff)
                     (concrete-supplier)
                     ,select-supplier act)
    ... ))
```

In contrast to the `object-base`, the `process-base` remains constant during the course of the simulation run.

The following function `executable-processes`

```
(define executable-processes
  (lambda ()
    (filter (lambda (x)
              (let ([inputs (cadr x)])
                (subset inputs (map car object-base))))
            process-base)))
```

filters all processes from the `process-base` whose input objects `inputs` all have a counterpart in the `object-base`, i.e. for which

$$\text{inputs} \subseteq \text{(map car object-base)}$$

yields true. As aforementioned, only the process steps which are currently executable create a respective menu item at a given point in simulation time.

Top-Level Menus and Menu Items

Before describing the core algorithms of the process interpreter, we first need to explain the menu structure of the interactive simulation.

The top-level menus are marked with object-names (cf. figure 5.6, where the top-level menus are named "project-plan", "staff", "sw-product", "requirements", "request-for-proposal", and "concrete-supplier"). The actual

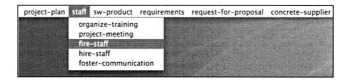

Figure 5.6.: Example menu structure of a process-oriented interactive simulation run

process steps the player can choose from are arranged in menu items. Each menu item is associated with a top-level menu and marked with the name of the respective process step function. The menu items are arranged in such a way that, under a menu marked with object type o, we can find all process step functions which generate or change an object of type o. So, the fact that the top-level menu "staff" is associated with the process steps functions "organize-training", "project-meeting", "fire-staff", "hire-staff", and "foster-communication" means the following:

1. All these process step functions are executable (otherwise they would not be visible); for all their formal input parameters, there exists an actual counterpart in the object-base.

2. All these process step functions have an object of type "staff" among their outputs.

There are, of course, other arrangements of the process step functions in a graphical user interface conceivable, and it is a more or less arbitrary decision to arrange them in the aforementioned way. This specific decision, however, is not crucial for our treatment; it hardly influences the overall design of the process interpreter.

Top level menus that have no associated menu items should not be visible to the player; the player should see solely objects in the menu bar for which an executable process step exists which has the respective object in his output list; expressed in terms of Scheme, this means that, for each tag o of a visible top-level menu, the following condition holds:

$$o \in \texttt{(apply append (map caddr (executable-processes)))}$$

Creating and Updating the Menu

The `create-menu-items` function is central to the implementation of the process interpreter. It instantiates all executable process step functions with respective objects from the object base and creates respective menu items associated with the respective top level menus.

```
(define create-menu-items
  (lambda ()
    (let ([menus (create-menus)])
      (map (lambda (x)
             (let* ([proc-name (symbol->string (car x))]
                    [proc-outputs (caddr x)]
                    [mk-menu-item
                      (lambda (obj-sym)
                        (make-object menu-item% proc-name
                          (cdr (assq obj-sym menus))
                          (instantiate-func x)))])
               (map mk-menu-item proc-outputs)))
           (executable-processes)))))
```

The underlying algorithm of `create-menu-items` functions via two nested maps. The outer `map` "runs" over all executable processes and creates for each one the respective menu items. The creation of the menu items is performed by the inner `map`, which applies the locally defined function `mk-menu-item` on each output object type of a specific process step. The function `mk-menu-item` gets an object type `obj-sym`, fetches the respective top level menu through

$$(cdr \ (assq \ obj-sym \ menus)),$$

creates a new menu item associated to the fetched menu, and links it with the instantiated process step function.

The instantiation is performed through the function `instantiate-func`:

```
(define instantiate-func
  (lambda (proc-tuple)
    (let ([inputs (map object-find (cadr proc-tuple))]
          [actual-proc (cadddr proc-tuple)])
      (lambda (x y)
        (let ([output (apply actual-proc inputs)])
```

```
(for-each object-insert output)
(update-messages)
(update-menus)
(update-menus-items)))))))
```

It gets as input an executable process step with its respective information in a 5-tuple `proc-tuple` and builds the procedure which is called when the player of the simulation selects the respective menu item. In detail, this is performed as follows: through mapping `object-find` over (`cadr proc-tuple`), i.e. over the 5-tuple's second component representing the list of input object types, it stores the actual objects which correspond to the formal input parameters of the process step function in the `inputs` variable. Note that all these objects exist since the process step is executable. The actual process step function is the fourth component of the 5-tuple, i.e. (`cadddr proc-tuple`); it is stored in the local variable `actual-proc`.

`Instantiate-func` is higher-order; its result is a special *callback* procedure which can be associated with a menu item and which is called when the player selects this menu item. For technical reasons, it has to be a function of two arguments which are not used in our case, however. The variable `output` is crucial; it stores the results of the process step function applied to its actual parameters (stored in `inputs`), i.e. `output` receives the value (`apply actual-proc inputs`). Note that we have a *lazy* semantics here: `output` receives its value not until the player selects the respective menu item.

Process step functions return lists of objects, and the command (`for-each object- insert output`) inserts all elements of `output` in the `object-base`. This can change the set of executable processes, and the menu structure has to be updated. The function `update-menu-items` does basically the same as `create-menu-items`; it additionally deletes menu items whose corresponding process step function looses their "executable" property.

5.5. Detailed Simulation Design Using Best Practice Information

So far, we described the simulation's skeleton. The art, however, lies in filling it with live, that is, in providing detailed implementations for the process step functions, as indicated by figure 5.4, and in determining the objects' attributes, the relationships between objects, and the objects' dynamical behavior. Although these issues are not directly in scope – this research deals with combining process steps functions to an interactive simulation and not with the detailed design of the process step functions themselves – we sketch how to move the "art", at least partially, into an engineering task. We suggest to systematically use best practice information – particularly information in GARP's best practice framework – for the detailed design of the process step functions.

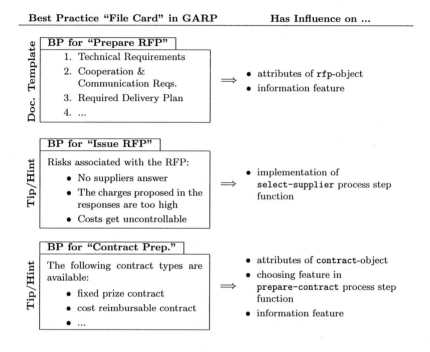

Figure 5.7.: Examples for using best practice information in building the interactive simulation

As described in section 3.2.3, GARP divides best practices in information kinds. We will consider two information kinds here: *tips and hints* and *document templates.* Figure 5.7 shows examples of template and tip-and-hint best practices and how they influence and help in the detailed design of the simulation.

Document templates influence the designer's decision about object attributes since templates provide a structure – and thus characteristics – of an object. The tip-and-hints – two examples of them are shown in figure 5.7

– can be quite diverse by their nature. One tip-and-hint indicates the risks which could be associated with the request for proposal. This influences the design of the subsequent process step function `select-supplier` because it is the point, where the risks can occur. A best practice which points out what types of contract exist could influence the design of the `contract`-object's attributes, and it could lead to an extension of the `prepare-contract` process step function with a *choose feature*, which lets the player select a contract type and/or an *information feature*.

5.6. Validity and Soundness

The process interpreter's compilation of process steps can be seen as a different representation of the same concepts used in GARP, namely the process combinators. The question of the validity of the process-oriented interactive simulation is closely related with the question if the representation of the process combinators is coherent to our intuition what this representation expresses or, in other words, it is closely related with the question if this representation is sound. And in fact, through this interpretation mechanism, temporal ordering, concurrency, and non-determinacy of process steps are properly expressed: the player "perceives" the temporal ordering through the dynamic change of the menus in the course of the simulation, the concurrency through the possibility to choose the execution order of process steps, and the non-determinacy through the possibility to choose exactly one alternative.

A more exhaustive validation would entail a complete implementation of an interactive software acquisition simulation which we, however, omit in the context of this dissertation. The reasons are unreasonable costs for a complete implementation. And even if we had a complete implementation of such a simulation, we would gain little (compared to the high implementation costs) through this since an implementation would merely provide another indicator – no proof – for the validity of this simulation technique. Furthermore, the question remains how to test the validity of that interactive simulation (should it, for instance, be realistic or just useful from an educational point of view). We need a complex machinery for all this and thus decide to leave further validation to future work.

5.7. Concluding Remarks and Future Work

In this chapter, we seek to build simulation games representing a software acquisition project; such games are usually called *interactive process simulations* – the player of the game takes the role of a project manager and closely interacts with the simulation. This chapter presented a novel approach to interactive software process simulation. The approach is called *process-oriented*; a process builds the basis for the simulation, and GARP or any similar process model is easily mappable to such an interactive simulation.

5.7.1. The Gaps of the Framework

This approach is presented as a (kind of) functional framework in the programming language Scheme. It determines the design of process steps and how they can be combined into an interactive simulation. However, the framework provides neither guidelines how to realize the process steps in detail, nor methods how to represent the project dynamics.

There are no fixed techniques to fill these gaps, but, for several reasons, System Dynamics seems an appropriate method to describe the project dynamics; in chapter 9, we show how to use System Dynamics to describe the dynamics of a process-oriented interactive simulation.

5.7.2. Possible Future Enhancements

A drawback in the presented simulation framework is, however, that knowledge in writing Scheme functions is required in order to be able to build interactive simulations. Future extensions should provide facilities to build simulations without programming knowledge. The future GUI should enable the user to build a customized interactive simulation solely through mouse clicks. But actually, this is not an enhancement of the framework but rather a particular sophisticated instance of the framework.

A real enhancement of the concepts presented in this chapter, however, would be the development of a multi-player interactive simulation with one player taking the role of the management of the software acquisition project and the other players taking the roles of managers of the respective suppliers' software development teams; thereby, the dynamics of acquisition projects could be clarified even better. The multi-player version would allow to play *against* each other which increases the players' fun and motivation, and it emphasizes the nature of software acquisition: each side wants to get out the most for themselves; from an educational perspective, a good game design should show the players that this is possible only when the partners cooperate rather than compete.

5.7.3. Spatial Interactive Simulation

We call interactive simulation games *spatial* when the following two conditions hold:

1. The simulation is, in a sense, three-dimensional. Not only the time is simulated but also the space in which the simulated part of reality takes place.

2. At a given point in the simulated time, (most, not all) simulated objects have a defined position in the simulation space.

Figure 5.8.: An example of a possible space-based interactive simulation of a software (acquisition) project.

Many commercial interactive simulation games are *spatial*. An example is SimCity where the player is mayor and seeks to let his city grow and flourish.

The city's space and the surrounding landscape is simulated, and streets houses, plots, commercial centers, and most other simulated objects have a well-defined position in the space at a given point in simulated time.

The spatial interactive simulation approach is clearly orthogonal to the process-oriented approach; they can both be combined and exist on their own possibly in combination with other paradigms like microsimulation or System Dynamics. However, no spatial interactive simulation of software projects is described in literature – at least as far as the author knows. This would allow a simulation to move closer to reality. A spatial simulation system would lay the ground for the description of project dynamics which is closer to reality than the established description methods like System Dynamics or SESAM's underlying rule-based system. Figure 5.8 shows a possible scenario of a spatial software process simulation game. Restructuring the office – DeMarco's peopleware book [19] might be the source for respective simulation rules – watching people work, talk, argue, etc. are only a few new possibilities arising from spatial software process simulations.

Part III.

System Dynamics Simulation

Part II deals with a simulation method which has a clearly specified process consisting of the sequential, concurrent, and iterative combination of process steps as fundament. This part treats the modeling and simulation of software acquisition projects from a substantially different angle: *System Dynamics* [30, 66] is used to simulate software acquisition processes. Why do we switch to another simulation paradigm? The interactive approach described in chapter 5 is simple and well-worth for giving the player a taste of the process as a whole. However, in order to measure up to the complex dynamics of many process steps in software acquisition – for instance, the "management", "supplier monitoring", and "supplier controlling" process steps, whose efficient and successful performance is crucial to the success of an acquisition project –, we need more appropriate ways to characterize these process steps. Their dynamics adheres to the typical "actual state → perceived state → resulting pressures" loop. Systems whose dynamics adhere to this characteristic loop can, according to Robertson and Pugh [66], ideally be described through system dynamics modeling and simulation.

The interactive approach lacks ability to express complex dynamic rules of project behavior, whereas System Dynamics is especially made for this. System Dynamics can describe the behavior of processes whose basis is a set of dynamic rules which are true for the whole time. However, actions that are solely performed once and whose intrinsic behavior is not determined by feedback loops like the process steps "tendering" or "supplier selection" cannot be sensibly modeled in System Dynamics. But this is exactly what the interactive simulation method was made for. In this respect, the interactive simulation approach of chapter 5 and System Dynamics perfectly complement one another, and an adequate combination of them – if it exists at all – thus promises to be fruitful. Part IV deals with the question if and how the two approaches could be integrated.

Chapter 6 introduces techniques used in the rest of part III, namely the system dynamics philosophy and notation. It additionally introduces alternative simulation methods and justifies the decision to use System Dynamics in our context. We capture the common structures of system dynamics models of the software acquisition process through developing a model framework in chapter 7. It is the basis for chapter 8, which presents the development of a concrete model.

Chapter 6

System Dynamics and Alternatives

System Dynamics began as Forrester's "Industrial Dynamics" [29] in 1961. Its underlying assumption is that human mind is excellent in observing the elementary forces and actions (like pressures, fears, habits, prejudices, delays, resistance to change, greed, and many other characteristics influencing systems, specially human systems) of which a system is composed. But as human experience is poor for estimating the dynamic consequences of how the system's parts will interact with one another, computer simulation should be used here. There is a growing awareness that the behavior in biological, environmental, industrial, and societal systems can be appropriately modeled with System Dynamics and feedback systems.

After giving a few statements about System Dynamics' underlying ideas and philosophy in section 6.1, section 6.2 introduces the model types and their syntactic structures. Section 6.3 deals with the process of system dynamics modeling. Following Richardson and Pugh's advice how to save one from "having to think about everything in order to think about something"

–

> "Two very broad guidelines are helpful in reducing the complexity of the problem definition and conceptualization phases: (1) have a clear purpose for the modeling effort. (2) focus on a problem, not on a system" [66]

– section 6.4 deals with the model purpose in general and the modeling purpose specific for this modeling project. (The actual problems to be modeled can be found in the next chapter in section 7.1.)

6.1. Central Tenets Underlying System Dynamics

A postulate in system sciences and particularly in System Dynamics – probably the most fundamental one – is that structure causes behavior or, in other words, that dynamic behavior is a consequence of system structure. Here, "structure" means the subsystems and entities a system is composed of and their mutual relationships.

A fundamental structural building block is the feedback loop (cf. section 6.2.2). System Dynamics assumes that feedback structures are the main determinants of the behavior of a system, and the goal of the system dynamics approach is actually the understanding of feedback systems. This assumption is both: a consequence *and* a cause for the internal view on problems: System Dynamics tends to look within a system for sources of its problem behavior, and problems are not seen as being caused by external agents outside the system; the system boundary is drawn accordingly: external agents, at least the ones which are important for the system behavior, are brought inside the system boundary.

So, the focus on feedback structures and the internal view on problems are actually two sides of the same coin:

- The internal view entails the focus on feedback structures: the internal view forces one to search for the causes and effects of a variable *inside* the system; the modeler is forced to bring missing links (of loops) to the interior which necessarily leads to a focus on loops.

- On the other hand, the focus on feedback structures entails an internal view: since the causal links of a feedback loop never leave the system boundary (and the system boundary should be defined in a way that they do not leave it), the focus on loops entails an internal view on problems.

6.2. Technical Introduction

This subsection (informally) describes the syntax and semantics of System Dynamics' two diagram types: the flow graphs and the causal loop diagrams which are similar to the flow graphs but simpler and less expressible: flow graphs differentiate between material flows and causal links whereas causal loop diagrams do not.

6.2.1. Causal Loop Diagrams

Causal loop diagrams are directed graphs whose edges may be – but need not be – labeled either with a plus or a minus sign. The vertices are sloppily called "variables"; they are factors which are considered relevant for system behavior. The edges are called "causal links"; they indicate that there is some kind of causal influence of one variable on another. Figures 6.1, 6.2, 7.2, and 7.3 provide examples for causal loop diagrams.

A causal link labeled with a plus sign is called "positive", and a causal link labeled with a minus sign is called "negative". Labeled edges provide information about the type of causality. A positive link indicates that the variables at the opposite ends of the edge tend to move in the same direction. For example the link from "motivation" to "effectiveness" in figure 6.2 is positive, since we suppose that an increase in motivation entails an increase in effectiveness. And the link from "workforce" to "production" in figure 6.1 is positive, since we suppose that a greater workforce (usually) entails an increase in production.

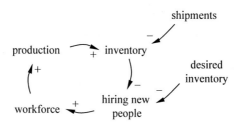

Figure 6.1.: An example negative causal loop

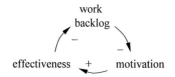

Figure 6.2.: An example positive causal loop

A minus sign indicates the reverse relationship: the variables linked with the edge tend to move in opposite directions. For example the link from "effectiveness" to "work backlog" in figure 6.2 is negative, since a decrease in effectiveness entails an increase in the work backlog (and vice versa) and the link from "shipments" to "inventory" in figure 6.1 is negative, since a decrease in shipments increases the inventory or, at least, makes the inventory decrease slower.

6.2.2. Feedback

Feedback means the transmission and return of information, and a feedback loop is a closed sequence of causes and effects, a closed path of action and information. As indicated in section 6.1, feedback loops are crucial to the behavior of system dynamics models, and so they are treated in a separate section here.

There are two primary types of feedback: *positive* loops and *negative* loops. If a cycle contains an even number of negative links, then the cycle represents a positive feedback loop, whereas an odd number of negative links represents a negative feedback loop. Negative feedback loops are goal-seeking loops; they are trying to find an equilibrium. The negating property can be demonstrated by placing a change around the loop. The variables are "swinging" back and forth around the equilibrium like a pendulum, finally reaching the equilibrium. Figure 6.1 shows an example of a negative feedback loop which tries to keep the inventory at its desired level.

Positive feedback loops do not necessarily oscillate like a pendulum. They are rather destabilizing, disequilibrating, growth-producing, or self-reinforcing. They are often experienced as vicious circles. Figure 6.2 shows an example of a positive feedback loop: an increase in the work backlog finally leads again to an increase in the work backlog, since it makes motivation and also effectiveness drop.

In more complex models, we usually have to deal with an interconnected system of feedback loops, and we are interested in its behavior. When a feedback loop is within another loop, one loop must dominate in terms of the overall behavior. Stable conditions will exist when negative loops dominate positive loops.

The behavior of single isolated feedback loops is usually intuitively clear. The behavior of a system of interconnected feedback loops, however, tends to get complex and often misguides our intuition about its behavior. We need simulation in order to explore its behavior.

6.2.3. System Dynamics Flow Graphs

Figures 6.3, 7.4, 7.6, 7.7, 7.8, and 7.9 provide examples of system dynamic flow graphs. In contrast to causal loop diagrams, they differentiate between information links and physical links, and the notion of accumulation is treated explicitly. One reason for this is that the equations one uses to model accumulations quantitatively are different from ordinary algebraic relationships.

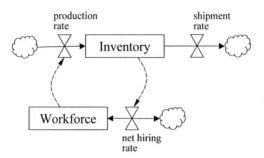

Figure 6.3.: A simple system dynamics flow graph

In System Dynamics, accumulations are called "levels" – intended to invoke the image of the level of a liquid accumulating in a container. They are graphically represented in rectangles, which are meant as stylized tubs. Figure 6.3 shows two level variables: "workforce" and "inventory". The flows increasing and decreasing a level are called "rates", depicted as stylized valves – this also emphasizes the analogy to the flow of a liquid. In figure 6.3 the "production rate" controls the increase, and the "shipment rate" controls the decrease of the "inventory"-level, and the "net hiring rate" controls the decrease and increase of the "workforce"-level. Generally speaking, rates (or rate equations respectively) translate planning and system pressures into actions altering the state of the system.

The cloud-like symbols represent sources and sinks for the material (whatever that is) flowing into and out of the level, and they are showing the system boundary: for the system behavior, it is neither relevant what will happen with the "material" after it flowed into a sink, nor is it relevant what happened before it flows out of a source. The notation clearly differentiates between physical and information flows: material flows are drawn as solid arrows, whereas causal links are drawn as dotted arrows.

Yet there are pieces of information – neither levels nor rates – that we will want to name and understand in our feedback models. They are called "auxiliaries" or "auxiliary variables". The model shown in figure 6.3 is very simple and provides no examples for using auxiliaries, but the system dynamics model (or respective fragments of it) of software acquisition projects presented in later sections uses them extensively. Although some auxiliaries might appear to represent an accumulation in the system, like, for instance, the auxiliaries denoting "progress" in figure 7.7, they have more in common with rate equations than with levels.

A model with fully quantified links, flows, rates, levels, and auxiliaries can be translated into a set of differential equations, which can then be simulated according to the rules for difference equations.

6.3. The Modeling Process

Due to Richardson and Pugh [66] there are basically the following stages of the system dynamics modeling process:

1. **Problem Definition**: The main purpose of system dynamics models is to illustrate a set of questions or problems related to the respective system, and in the problem definition phase these questions are determined. Section 7.1 provides a list of the respective problems. Equally important is the definition of the problems' dynamics in terms of graphs of variables over time, which are called *reference behavior modes*; these can also be found in section 7.1.

2. **Model Conceptualization**: Due to Richardson and Pugh [66], the conceptualization phase comprises the definition of the system boundary and the basic feedback structures. They assume, however, that the goal is to model one specific system, whereas our modeling effort aims to be more generic. Our conceptualization phase comprises the development of a model framework, described in section 7.4, which can be adapted – as we claim in section 7.6 – to (nearly) any specific software acquisition project scenario.

3. **Model Formulation**: This usually comprises the coding of the feedback structures into an executable simulation model (in DYNAMO, Vensim , or a similar simulation system). In this work, the "model formulation" step comprises two activities: first, the adaption and tailoring of the framework to a concrete project scenario, and, second, the actual quantification and coding of the model (here: in Vensim).

These issues about model formulation are discussed in sections 8.2 and 8.3.

4. **Simulation and Evaluation**: The last stage in a system dynamics modeling project is the simulation and the evaluation of the respective outputs. This is treated in section 8.5.

6.4. Modeling Purposes in System Dynamics

In constructing a useful dynamic model of a system's behavior, it is essential to have clearly in mind the purposes of the model. A clear understanding of the purposes of a modeling effort helps to answer questions concerning the system boundary. The modeler can hardly decide which part of reality should be excluded and which part should be included without referring to the modeling purposes.

6.4.1. General Modeling Purposes

One purpose might be to test a theory in the form of assumptions about feedback structures of a given system. Relevant in such a modeling effort is the question, if these assumptions can create a certain pattern of behavior over time.

A more common purpose, however, is prediction and to give quantitative prognoses on certain variables and their behavior over time. The requirement for such models is that they should be able to generate the so-called *reference behavior modes* – graphs of important variables over time. These variables should specify clearly the problematic behavior of the system we are interested in. They should – but often cannot, as Richardson and Pugh [66] note – be based on actual data:

> "It [the modeling process] does not require, as some might expect, that the modeler have access to explicit numerical data or well-defined functions to graph. While data is very helpful, one is often faced with a dynamic problem in which a key variable is not traditionally quantified or tabulated. It is even more likely, however, that the modeler or the client knows the dynamic behavior of interest without referring to data." [66], page 19

It is nearly impossible to collect data about both actual *and* perceived states of a certain part of the system, and we also cannot expect exact data about hardly measurable factors like "pressure" or "trust" – in these cases, we have to trust experience. The model's ability to generate the reference modes is seen as an indicator that it can predict what would happen, if another policy is employed or if decision making would be changed in certain aspects.

Less ambitious system dynamics projects are solely seeking to illustrate the consequences of certain assumptions about the dynamics of a system. Specially when the assumptions are parts of a complex circular structure, the consequences are far from being obvious and are sometimes even far from being intuitive. Computer simulation of system dynamics models is an excellent means to illustrate the dynamic consequences and serves as a tool to experiment with implications of different policies. Note, however, that the implications only reflect reality when the assumptions of the system's dynamics are reasonable.

6.4.2. Our Modeling Purposes

The system dynamics project described here is – at least with respect to its requirements on exact predictions – less ambitious, and the purposes correspond to what is written in the last paragraph of section 6.4.1. The profits we expect from this system dynamics modeling effort are the following:

- Due to the underestimation of an acquisition project's complexity and risk, we need a way to raise consciousness among decision makers (like project managers and even higher management of a firm).

- The interactive simulation approach is well suited for giving an impression of the functioning of the overall acquisition project. However, it can hardly express the complex dynamics of continuous process steps like "project management" or "supplier monitoring". So, we have to look at other simulation paradigms whose expressive power can cope with these complex dynamics and employ System Dynamics for this purpose.

We do *not* understand "simulation" in the sense of exact prediction of project scenarios, given a set of initial conditions, but rather in the sense of an illustration of problems, e.g. "What could happen if I decide to do A?" or "How could I best influence B?". We do not seek to detect any laws of nature or the ultimate truth behind software acquisition. We solely have to look for simulation methods and models whose results are sufficiently close to reality. The aim here is not to build a model which quantitatively reflects the real project exactly but to build a model which reflects the project

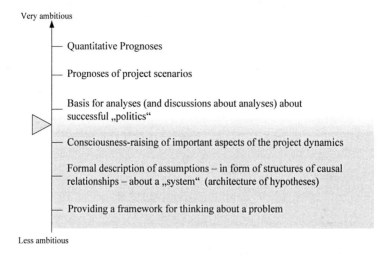

Very ambitious

— Quantitative Prognoses

— Prognoses of project scenarios

— Basis for analyses (and discussions about analyses) about
  successful „politics"

— Consciousness-raising of important aspects of the project dynamics

— Formal description of assumptions – in form of structures of causal
  relationships – about a „system" (architecture of hypotheses)

— Providing a framework for thinking about a problem

Less ambitious

Figure 6.4.: A list of modeling purposes in System Dynamics sorted by ambitiousness. The modeling purposes of the framework and its instances are put in gray.

structurally. We need a tool that allows clients to experiment with different policies for improving the management of a software acquisition project and see the results following directly from the (agreed) assumptions about software acquisition projects (partly in the form of causal feedback structures).

6.5. Why System Dynamics?

As aforementioned, one purpose of our simulation project is to raise consciousness about specific aspects in the dynamics of an acquisition project, and we can thus justify the decision to choose System Dynamics through its suitability to serve as a consciousness-raising tool.

There are two conceivable approaches for a consciousness-raising simulation, which should demonstrate the dynamics of management-like process steps. *Microanalytical simulation models* [14, 34] adhere to a bottom-up perspective; just "small" things are simulated, and the focus is on the emergent behavior resulting from micro behavior. Example representatives in the software process simulation world are the SESAM model [50] or an approach to simulate a requirements development process [13]. Microanalytical models, however, tend to get complex, and thus are less suited for concise presentations to decision makers. Thus, system dynamics simulation is a more appropriate method for the above mentioned purposes.

Another important reason to choose System Dynamics here is that, in contrast to other simulation approaches, System Dynamics' main goal is understanding the behavior of feedback systems. This qualifies it to be a reasonable method for describing acquisition projects, since feedback mechanisms are omnipresent there; examples are:

- the acquirer's attitude towards the supplier changes the supplier's attitude towards the acquirer, and the resulting effects on the project's effectiveness again influences the acquirer's attitude towards the supplier

- the acquirer's technological knowledge has influence on the effectiveness and quality in performing joint quality assurance activities with the supplier; the quality and the frequency of these activities in turn determine the growth of the acquirer's technological knowledge.

More feedback structures of acquisition projects can be found in section 7.4.

There is a second purpose for these simulation activities: we search for a simulation method which is suitable to supplement the interactive simulation method presented in chapter 5. System Dynamics also fits this purpose: the interactive simulation approach lacks ability to describe complex dynamic rules of project behavior whereas System Dynamics is perfectly suited for this. However, actions whose intrinsic behavior is not determined by feedback loops cannot be described in System Dynamics whereas the interactive simulation method is suited for this. In these respects, the interactive simulation method and System Dynamics perfectly complement each other. Section 9 shows that System Dynamics is indeed properly combinable with the process-oriented interactive simulation method.

6.6. Alternative Simulation Methods

Simulation of human systems is hard when the modeler is forced to reduce all aspects of a system to numeric form. This section shortly reviews two alternative modeling and simulation methods which promise – at least, at first glance – to remedy this shortcoming, i.e. which promise to overcome the strict quantification which system dynamics modeling prescribes. For each alternative, we justify our preference to (classical) System Dynamics.

6.6.1. Bayesian Networks

Bayesian networks – a concept from artificial intelligence – have similar structure than system dynamics models. They could therefore be taken into account as an alternative to System Dynamics for modeling and simulation of software acquisition projects.

Bayesian Networks – A Brief Overview

A Bayesian network models the probability distribution of various (dependent) events. Bayesian networks are a graphical representation of (in)dependencies amongst random variables. A Bayesian network is a directed acyclic graph with nodes representing random variables (which may also contain hypotheses about possible values of that variable) and arcs representing direct influence. The independence that is encoded in a Bayesian network is that each variable is independent of its non-descendents given its parents.

One can look at Bayesian networks as a story. An example is a story containing five random variables: "Burglary", "Earthquake", "Alarm", "Neighbor Call", and "Radio Announcement". Regarding the dependencies among these five events, we can represent this "story" as the Bayesian network shown in figure 6.5.

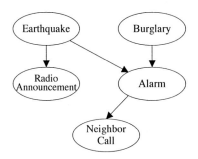

Figure 6.5.: A simple Bayesian Network.

Bayesian Networks are specially important in the field of artificial intelligence and artificial learning. They support complex inference modeling including rational decision making systems, value of information and sensitivity analysis. Bayesian networks are applied to a lesser extent for simulation; they are rather appropriate to support pattern recognition. NASA gathers data from deep-space observations and planetary probes; an a priori imposition of structure or pattern expectations is often not possible, since researchers do not know what to expect; they often even do not have hypotheses for which to test when gathering data. Through Bayesian networks, it is possible to construct own potential systems of meaning and a new classification upon the data (cf. the AutoClass project [11]).

A more prominent example for the application of Bayesian nets is the Lumiere project [39] at Microsoft. Its goal was to create software that could automatically and intelligently interact with users by anticipating their goals and needs. Lumiere finally resulted – with the launch of Office 95 products – in Microsoft's Office Assistant.

Applicability of Bayesian Networks in Our Context

Although the structure of Bayesian networks seems to be similar to the structure of causal loop diagrams (cf. section 6.2.1) and thus similar to the structure of system dynamics models, the meaning and the applicability of Bayesian networks greatly differ from the meaning and applicability of system dynamics models: Bayesian networks model uncertainty, and their goal is the determination of the probability that specific events occur. On the other hand, system dynamics models do *not* model uncertainty, and their goal is the determination of the impact of certain dynamic hypotheses.

So, if we want to know, whether Bayesian networks are an appropriate representation method for software acquisition processes, we should ask, if we have to model uncertainty. But in our approach to questions and problems regarding software acquisition, we are *not* uncertain that specific events occur: we know, for instance, that requirements will be implemented, we know that the progress will be perceived and respective actions will be taken, and we know that the acquirer's knowledge will grow while performing common quality assurance. What we do not know, in contrast, is the exact quantification of most variables and relationships; we solely are able to *roughly* reduce our hypotheses to numeric form. What seems more promising in a situation where we have diffuse data for rigid models are concepts from *fuzzy theory*.

6.6.2. Fuzzy System Dynamics

Another related research direction worth mentioning is that of fuzzy System Dynamics [23, 48, 65].

In quantitative simulation approaches, such as System Dynamics, all aspects to be included in the simulation must be reduced to numeric form. When it comes to simulating human systems such as software projects or software acquisition projects, however, the available information on which the simulation should be based, is imprecise, incomplete, and occasionally unreliable.

It has been tried to overcome this problem by using concepts of fuzziness in system dynamics modeling. After shortly introducing some concepts of fuzzy systems, we describe how these concepts have been used in system dynamics simulation. Finally, we justify the decision to stick to conventional system dynamics simulation in examining the dynamics of software acquisition.

Fuzziness

In the unfuzzified world, the membership of an element in a set can definitely be decided through a two-valued membership function which yields one, when the element is a member of the set, and zero otherwise. The fuzzified world, in contrast, provides membership functions which may yield arbitrary values in the interval $[0, 1]$.

More formally, a set

$$A = \{(x, f_A(x)) \mid x \in X\}, \text{ where } f_A : X \to [0, 1]$$

is called a *fuzzy set* on X. If there is exactly one m with $f_A(m) = 1$, if the fuzzy set A is convex, if $X = \mathbb{R}$ holds, and if f_A is piecewise continuous then A is a *fuzzy number*; m is called *mean value* of the fuzzy number A. Figure 6.6 shows an example of a fuzzy number with mean value 10 representing a value "around 10".

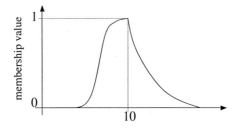

Figure 6.6.: An example of a fuzzy number.

Fuzziness is *not*, as often misunderstood, just another way to express randomness; fuzziness and randomness rather represent orthogonal aspects of the world. Fuzziness describes *event ambiguity*; it measures the degree to which an event occurs, *not* whether it occurs. Fuzziness is the right description method if we cannot – or if we do not want to – unambiguously distinguish the event from its opposite. Randomness, on the other hand, describes the uncertainty of event occurrence; it is the right description method, if we are not certain whether the event will actually occur.

The probably most often used feature of fuzzy systems is their ability to realize complex nonlinear input - output relations as a synthesis of multiple simple input/output relations. Ambiguity is artificially introduced here, in order to easily deal with complex relationships. In contrast to this, we examine fuzziness as a possibility to treat ambiguity inherent in human systems.

Fuzziness In Software Project Simulation With System Dynamics

Models of projects, particularly models of software acquisition projects, incorporate many hardly quantifiable variables like, for instance, "pressure", "trust", and variables representing perceptions. It seems straightforward to represent these variables as fuzzy numbers and use fuzzy logic and fuzzy arithmetic to determine the respective relationships. This means that – as usual in fuzzy theory – linguistic terminology is used to describe these unquantifiable variables; pressure would no longer be classified by a numeric value, but by a linguistic term like "low", "moderate", and "high".

There are basically two options to use fuzziness in System Dynamics:

1. The regular (i.e. non-fuzzy) versions of system dynamics tools for simulating software processes are used. The fuzzy input variables are handled by an external expert system, and the simulation results will also be handled by an output expert system having fuzzy logic. Levary and Lin [48] use this technique. In literature, however, there are hardly any experiences described about the usefulness of this technique and the validity of the respective models.

2. An extended system dynamics methodology can be developed and used capable of treating vague input variables, using fuzzy arithmetic in rate, level, and auxiliary equations and treating, in addition to conventional relationships, conditional relationships using fuzzy variables or fuzzy algorithms. Fatehi [22, 23] uses this technique. But, like in the case of Levary's and Lin's technique, there is no justification that this

technique yields more useful results than the classical system dynamics approach.

Applicability of Fuzziness in Our Context

We do not use any concept of fuzzy theory in modeling and simulating software acquisition projects. This has several reasons. First, both aforementioned techniques to use fuzziness in System Dynamics seem to be immature; no real experiences are reported in literature, and they still await validation in real-world scenarios. One could argue: "if the fuzzy system dynamics methodology is still not thoroughly validated – why is this not done here? Wouldn't this be an interesting research direction?". The answer is: yes, this would definitely be interesting, but it is not the focus of this dissertation. It is just one part of this dissertation which treats system dynamics simulation, and only one section of this part deals with the development of a concrete system dynamics model; it seems not reasonable to use an unestablished technique for a rather minor matter in this dissertation. Apart from this, since the framework described in chapter 7 abstracts from the concrete realization of respective simulation models, it is a basis for classical *and* fuzzy system dynamics models.

Additionally, there is a more fundamental reason why we stick to the classical system dynamics simulation: the author doubts the superiority of fuzzy system dynamics to classical System Dynamics. The focus in System Dynamics is on behavior *patterns* over time; the focus is usually not on exact prediction. While it might appear thoroughly to fuzzify hardly quantifiable variables (like pressure, trust, and all associated auxiliaries, and rate variables; like the variables representing perception and the "needs for ..."-variables), it is questionable, if one can obtain more insight through a fuzzification: it would simply smooth the output graphs of the system dynamics model – but this is exactly what our human perception does automatically when we focus on *rough* patterns over time.

We thus stick to classical system dynamics simulation in chapter 8, and this work shows, indeed, that valid models of the software acquisition process can be built with unfuzzified System Dynamics (cf. section 7.7 and 8.6).

6. System Dynamics and Alternatives

Chapter 7

Common Structures in System Dynamics Models of Software Acquisition Projects

The author does not know of any prior research in system dynamics modeling of software acquisition projects, and we face the problem of starting "from scratch" in model design. Additionally, in the software project simulation literature, there seems to be a lack of research in the methodical design of system dynamics models. So, the objective of this chapter is actually twofold:

Methodical design of system dynamics models. In consequence of Abdel-Hamid and Madnick's work [1], a large number of papers about the simulation of software processes using the system dynamics approach have been published. However, there is still a lack of research on the actual model design, specially on the design of software process models from scratch. But model design from scratch is exactly what we need to do here, since software acquisition is still an unexplored domain in system dynamics modeling. So, in this chapter, we want to – at least partly – remedy this lack. Section 7.3 presents

1. an approach for a more methodical and rigid design of system dynamics models, namely through the development of a model framework[1] for a certain domain and

---

[1] Unfortunately, the term "framework" is already heavily used in computer science, mostly in connection with object-oriented systems where "framework" means

"[...] a set of classes that embodies an abstract design for solutions to a number of related problems." [28]

One might think that we run the risk of misunderstandings when employing a term which is also used in object-oriented programming. But there are good reasons for using the term "framework" in this context: we need to name "a set of level, rate, and auxiliary variables that embodies an abstract model for a number of related systems"

2. a design strategy for such model frameworks.

Developing a system dynamics framework for acquisition projects.
There is hardly any prior work on the simulation of software acquisition projects. Therefore, before developing concrete models, we create a fundament through designing a framework which should capture the most important common structures of system dynamics models of software acquisition projects. The framework itself is formulated in the system dynamics notation.

Through the specification of the problems and the problem behavior to be modeled in section 7.1, we lay the groundwork for the subsequent material. Section 7.2 treats related work and shows that there is hardly any simulation tailored to software acquisition described in literature, and that there is in fact no prior work on system dynamics modeling of software acquisition projects.

Section 7.4 is the central section in this chapter; it describes the design of the framework based on the design principles treated in section 7.3. Through comparing the scope of the framework with the scope of Abdel-Hamid and Madnick's model [1] in section 7.5, we complete the material presented in section 7.4 through adding to the framework a system dynamics fragment representing human resource management activities. In section 7.6, we treat the question, how universal and adaptable the framework is – these are crucial questions, since we seek to build a framework applicable to *any* software acquisition project. Section 7.7 analyzes the validity of the framework, and section 7.8 concludes the chapter with final remarks.

7.1. Problems and Problem Behavior

In contrast to microanalytical models, System Dynamics adheres to a top-down style of modeling. Starting from dynamic hypotheses – a rough statement of feedback structures that are conjectured to have the power to create (or contribute to) the problem – a more detailed integrated model is developed as a second step. It is this top-down view that makes the models easier to comprehend and to present.

---

and the term "framework" optimally captures this issue. Furthermore, we are treating no object-oriented concepts in this dissertation and thus are not running the risk of mixing the two meanings of "object-oriented framework" and "system dynamics framework".

The name "System Dynamics" is deceptive: the focus is not on a system – whatever that is – but on dynamic problems, which are expressible in terms of graphs of variables over time. As Forrester already pointed out in his earlier work, one models problems, *not* solutions in System Dynamics:

> "Only by knowing the questions to be answered, we can safely judge the pertinence of factors to include in or omit from the system formulation." [29]

So, our goal is to develop a framework for models which address a specific set of questions associated with supplier selection and customer-supplier interactions. Potential instabilities caused by specific supplier management, monitoring, or controlling techniques (or by the absence of any techniques, respectively) should be illustrated to the acquisition project's management and staff as impressively as possible. We list the most relevant questions together with the respective answers which we hope to receive from system dynamics simulation:

1. *Question*: How effective is regular communication with the supplier(s)?

   Expected Answer: More effective than possibly expected.

2. *Question*: What can be expected of common quality assurance activities such as common risk management or joint reviews?

   Expected Answer: More effective than possibly expected, but it might take some time to see benefit.

3. *Question*: Which consequences does the application of severe pressure on the supplier have, given delay in the delivery of software products?

   Expected Answer: The supplier could loose confidence, which possibly entails further delay in the project.

4. *Question*: Which consequences does an unheeding supplier selection process have?

   Expected Answer: This could have dramatic implications on project performance.

5. *Question*: The acquirer does not engineer himself, and thus runs the risk of loosing technological know-how. What consequences has knowledge depletion and which arrangements could prevent it?

   Expected Answer: Knowledge depletion results in worse capabilities in controlling and monitoring the supplier. Knowledge depletion could be prevented by common quality assurance activities with the supplier.

To further focus the modeling effort, Richardson and Pugh [66] suggest to clearly specify also, in addition to the actual problems to be modeled, the "problematic" behavior of the respective system in terms of graphs over time. These graphs are called *reference behavior modes*. We shall require that the models we develop be able to generate similar patterns over time. Reference behavior modes need not be based on actual numeric data. In fact, sometimes they even cannot be based on actual numeric data – it is hardly possible, for instance, to collect data about the reported, the perceived, *and* the actual progress in a project – but rather may be based on our experience about software acquisition projects.

Figure 7.1 shows two reference behavior modes for two different project scenarios having one thing in common (which is also common for many acquisition projects due to our experience): the expense which the supplier will need for software development is underestimated in the early phases of the software acquisition project. Figure 7.1(a) shows an unfavorable course of such a project in terms of actual, perceived (i.e. perceived by the acquirer), and reported (i.e. the information the supplier provides *to* the acquirer) progress. Experience shows that problematic and risky projects are characterized by a huge gap in the actual progress and the reported/perceived progress. The reasons for the extent of the gap between the reported data and the actual data could be:

- A lack of the supplier's trust or the supplier's general negative mindset towards the project. The consequence is that, although the supplier might perceive the gap between the actual and the desired progress, he reports what the acquirer wants to hear in order to avoid problems.

- Due to a lack of experience, the supplier's project management is simply not aware of this gap and thus not *able* to perceive the actual progress and the actual unclarities.

In reality, we often face a mixture of these two reasons.

A second issue shown in figure 7.1(a) is that, for quite a long time, the progress perceived by the acquirer is nearly the same like the progress reported by the supplier; reasons for this are typically a lack of technological and technical knowledge on the acquirer's side, too less communication, and too less common quality assurance activities. This has dramatic consequences: the acquirer's actions to mitigate the problems in the project's

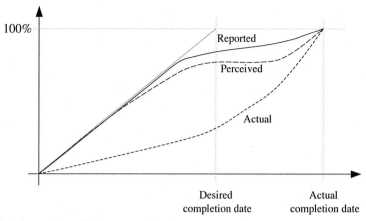

(a) An unfavorable course of a late acquisition project in terms of reported, perceived and actual progress.

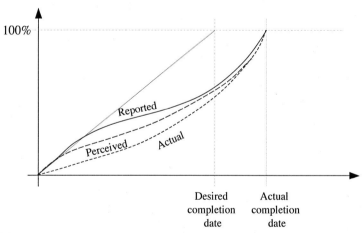

(b) A more favorable course of a late acquisition project in terms of reported, perceived and actual progress.

Figure 7.1.: Reference Behavior Modes

progress come late. Figure 7.1(a) shows that not until the acquirer notices the gap, the velocity of the actual progress rises.

A more favorable version of a late project's course shows figure 7.1(b). The progress perceived by the acquirer converges much earlier with the progress reported by the supplier. The reason might be a better technological understanding on the acquirer's side than in the project depicted in figure 7.1(a) or more involved monitoring and controlling techniques carried out by the acquirer. Another point is that the supplier is more willing – or more capable – to adapt his reports to reality. Consequence is that appropriate action to mitigate the project delay can be taken earlier which results in less retardation.

7.2. Related Work

In consequence of Abdel-Hamid and Madnick's pioneer work [1], a large number of papers about the simulation of software processes using the system dynamics approach appeared. Some of them [3, 15, 60, 71, 72, 83] present (parts of) their system dynamics models and try to legitimate – more or less sketchy – the models' structure on the basis of experience or known "rules" about software processes; and some [16, 51, 53] hardly do even that. Nearly all of these publications have in common that the actual way the authors achieve the model is not treated. There is a lack of research on model building guidelines.

There is a much smaller number of publications dealing with the simulation of software acquisition processes [12], and – to the author's knowledge – the area of *system dynamics* modeling of software acquisition projects has hardly been touched. There exists work on outsourcing decision support with the help of System Dynamics [52, 68]. However, the scope of the respective models reflects a long-term and organization-wide view on the acquisition of software and software related products. The questions they ask and the problems they model differ. They ask, "Given a certain market or organizational situation: is it advisable to outsource software development and maintenance in the long run?". On the other hand, we ask, "How can a *certain* software acquisition project be improved?".

7.3. The Model Design Approach

The structures of all system dynamics models of a certain domain are similar, and a rigid model design should take this into account. So, before developing concrete models in a new domain one should first think about common structures of these system dynamics models. Here, we capture common structures through the development of a *framework* (also expressed in system dynamics notation) for models of software acquisition projects. These structures are independent of concrete settings (like industry, project size, special type of contractual agreement, etc.); they have first to be instantiated in order to model a certain project. The development of a framework also accommodates the top-down nature of system dynamics modeling. In contrast to *microanalytical simulation models* [34], which simulate just "small" things and focus on the emergent behavior resulting from micro-behavior and thus adhere to a bottom-up perspective, system dynamics models are based on a system's structure and should be designed top-down (though this might be debatable, a top-down design is suggested by the relevant literature [66] and practiced, for example, by Forrester [31]).

We suggest to develop such frameworks – at least partially – *deductively*. Modern philosophers of science like Karl Popper [61] and Gregory Bateson [5] stress the importance of a deductive research style and the lack of todays research due to too much induction; "deductive" means that new insight is gained through inference from existing, possibly more abstract principles which are known to be true, or – at least in non-mathematical sciences – have been proven to be useful and reasonable. Note that "deduction" does not always need to mean "the *necessary* conclusion from general premises", as the online Merriam-Webster's dictionary defines it. This is true for logic or mathematics, but in "softer" fields of science like system dynamics modeling one rather should interpret "deduction" as "derivation of a conclusion by *informal* reasoning"; this is in accordance particularly with Gregory Bateson's view on "deduction".

In our case, we take well-approved research in similar application areas as a basis, namely Abdel-Hamid's and Madnick's model for software projects [1] and McCray's and Clark's model for the impacts of outsourcing [52] and "deduce" from them – either through analogy or antagonism and contrast – common (feedback) structures for acquisition projects. Of course, in order to design the framework, we also need to access observations and experience about acquisition projects, and thus the approach is a mixture of deduction and induction; however, it differs from other approaches by the fact that the deductive part is at least equally important.

7.4. A Software Acquisition Model Framework

The first two subsections are introductory. Section 7.4.1 discusses the framework's scope which differs from the scope of established models of the acquisition process like PULSE [64] or SA-CMM [17], and section 7.4.2 gives general remarks about the complexity of acquisition models. The remaining subsections present the actual framework; they adopt Forrester's style of model explanation (which he uses, for example, in his world model [31]): we present framework fragments in order to elaborately explain structure and feedback loops. The complete framework is finally shown at a glance in section 7.4.8.

7.4.1. Remarks on the Framework's Scope

According to established process models for software acquisition like the SA-CMM [17] or PULSE [64], we modeled just a part of the software acquisition process. The system dynamics framework focuses on the "supplier monitoring and controlling"-activity. The early phases of software acquisition projects like tendering, and supplier selection, as well as the their final phases like acceptance, integration, and maintenance are not considered in our model.

One reason for this is that the span determined by the problems mentioned in section 7.1 does not include acceptance, integration, and maintenance; and these problems determine the framework's scope. Another reason for these omissions is the inability of the system dynamics paradigm to model actions which are solely performed once like the tendering and the supplier selection; they do not adhere to uniform dynamic rules over a period of time, and their performance is not determined through intrinsic feedback loops. So, the supplier selection process is not modeled in our approach and problem 4 of section 7.1, asking which consequences an unheeding supplier selection process has, is not directly in scope. Nevertheless, this question can be "answered" through altering supplier specific parameters (like, for instance, the implementation rate, the supplier's comprehension rate, or the trust generation rate) representing a supplier chosen through an unheeding selection process.

7.4.2. Remarks on Complexity

According to Robertson and Pugh, there is a basic high level structure inherent in all system dynamics models:

> "Note that many decisions take a classic form: the actual state of the system, the perceived state of the system, a desired state, planning and pressures to close the gap, and resulting action changing the actual and perceived states of the system and closing a feedback loop"[66], page 63

and they further note:

> "Availability of information is a primary concern; the modeler must represent the information on which actors in the system actually base decisions."[66], page 63

Having this in mind, we take a look on the complexity inherent in the software acquisition process.

A reason why pure in-house ventures are less complex is that a further level of indirection is intrinsic to software acquisition projects: like in software development projects, we have to perceive the staff's progress, compare it to the desired progress and react accordingly. But the fact that the actions of the acquisition's staff are *controlling* the supplier's software development and thus managerial by their nature makes software acquisition intricate; compared to development projects we have to deal with one additional "actual state → perceived state → resulting pressures"-loop. This is shown in figure 7.2.

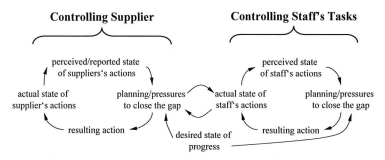

Figure 7.2.: The two controlling loops of the acquisition process.

There is another (but similar) reasonable angle to view the cause of higher complexity. In addition to the "perceive"-variables, we have to deal with a second source of subjectiveness: variables expressing the status *reported* by the supplier; figure 7.3 shows this in bold face. For obvious reasons,

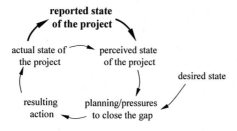

Figure 7.3.: additional element in acquisition loop.

the "subjective" variables have no simple cause and effect relationships but are highly enmeshed with the rest of the model and are therefore the most relevant sources for intricate and unpredictable behavior. Dealing with just one further root of subjectiveness entails a dramatic growth in complexity.

7.4.3. Models' Backbone

In the system dynamics modeling literature [30, 66], the term "backbone" does not exist, but we found it convenient to name the "matter" around which the process centers or, in other words, to name the actual outcome of the project or product to be built through the process. This "matter" or "product" is typically formed or built (i.e. it grows) in the course of the process, and in System Dynamics it is therefore modeled as a level variable or as a sequence of connected levels, since the "product" usually passes through several stages. Note, however, that using the term "backbone" makes sense solely in modeling targeted processes like, for instance, projects.

In software development projects, the backbone is clearly the software to be built, represented as "Lines of Code" or, as Abdel-Hamid and Madnick [1] suggest, as "Tasks". The left part of figure 7.4 shows their software process backbone and a small part of corresponding causal relationships forming the main feedback loop. Software is also central in the software acquisition process. But from an acquirer's point of view the focus is not on how in detail the software is produced. Rather more important is the question, if the requirements given to the supplier are complete, if they are understood by the supplier, and how many requirements are yet realized. This leads directly to the backbone shown in the right part of figure 7.4.

Note that this proceeding has a clear deductive flavor. First, we look at the patterns which well-proven models in similar domains exhibit and detect

Abdel-Hamid & Madnick's "Backbone" **Software Acquisition "Backbone"**

MDs remaining Productivity

WF-Level

SW Development Rate

Requirements still not considered

Acquirer's comprehension rate

Assumed Dev. Productivity

Tasks Developed

Reqs given to supplier (but still unclear to supplier)

Supp's comprehension rate

MDs perceived still needed for new tasks Errors

QA Rate

MDs perceived needed for rework

Tasks QAed

Reqs understood by supplier

Supp's implementation rate

Testing Rate

MDs perceived needed for testing

Tasks Tested

Reqs implemented

Figure 7.4.: Software process backbones

that all these models have a sequence of interconnected levels forming the center of the respective system. Then, we determine the shape that this pattern should reasonably have in our case.

7.4.4. Tasks

Abdel-Hamid and Madnick model the work of a software development project's staff as level variables called "Tasks", which are closely related with the developed software. We also choose to model staff's work as level variables called "Tasks", but since these acquisition tasks are *not* production but management and controlling activities, their representation differs as shown in figure 7.5. The levels representing engineering tasks are sequen-

Software Tasks   **Acquisition Tasks**

Figure 7.5.: Software tasks and software acquisition tasks

tially ordered because a production process usually consists of intermediate stages. In order to avoid any confusion, note the following: this does *not* at all imply that the respective project uses a waterfall software development process. Although the sequentially ordered levels do imply that a piece of software has first to be developed before it is tested, they do not imply that one piece of software cannot be developed while another piece is tested and a third piece is reworked. The system dynamics model of a software development project is not related to the software Life Cycle Framework[2] used in the project – like the system dynamics model of an acquisition project is not related to the respective acquisition Life Cycle Framework. System dynamics models abstract away the concrete life cycle processes.

After this little excursion into the relationship of system dynamics models and Life Cycle Frameworks, we go back to the modeling of acquisition tasks in system dynamics. While engineering tasks are sequentially ordered, acquisition tasks are concurrently ordered, since controlling and management are highly concurrent by their nature.

Design decisions in system dynamics modeling should be mainly influenced by the problems we want to illustrate. Referring to the first and second problem mentioned in chapter 7.1, we choose to differ between two kinds of tasks which are shown in figure 7.6: first, communication and coordination ac-

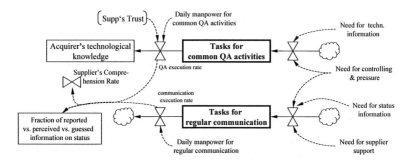

Figure 7.6.: Software acquisition tasks and their causal surroundings

tivities and, second, tasks concerning common quality assurance activities like, for instance, common risk management or common configuration management. They demand much more man-power than pure communication tasks, but provide benefits: the acquirer becomes partly independent from the supplier's reports and is able to collect more objective information about the status of the project; this fact is coded in the arrows going off the tasks' outflow rates. Furthermore, the acquirer increases his technological knowl-

---

[2]see section 2.2.2 for an explanation of the term "Software Life Cycle Framework"

edge, especially during joint reviews or audits. A lack of the supplier's trust, however, might considerably hamper the execution of joint quality assurance activities. Both kinds of tasks help the supplier in understanding requirements which are still unclear and thus increase the supplier's comprehension rate.

The tasks are involved in a big feedback loop (which is not explicitly shown in figure 7.6): the performance of the tasks, i.e. the outflow rates of the task levels, influences the quality of information about the project status gathered by the acquirer, which, in turn, affects decisions about the level of communication and common quality assurance henceforth.

Again, we proceeded deductively. We abstracted common patterns in well-proven models in similar domains of system dynamics modeling, namely the domain of software development. In this case, we derived our solutions not through analogy (as in the case of the last section about backbones) but through contrast: we considered differences between software development projects and software acquisition projects and derived respective differences in the modeling of tasks.

7.4.5. Perceiving and Reacting to the Backbone's Status

As Richardson and Pugh note, the distinction between reality and subjectiveness is crucial in System Dynamics:

> "The distinction between reality and the perception of reality is vitally important in system dynamics models – it might be said to be characteristic of them. The modeler must realize that not all the quantities represented in the model are knowable within the system being modeled. Some information is inaccessible to actors in the system." [66], page 58

A common pattern in the dynamics of targeted processes is the backbone (see section 7.4.3) and its embedding in the causal network: the backbone status is perceived and decisions about corresponding task levels, which in turn have influence on the backbone, are made. In the software development model, the task levels themselves form the backbone, and, thus, this loop, which is roughly shown in the left part of figure 7.4, is shorter and less complex than the analogous software acquisition loop.

Figure 7.7 shows that there are two different paths through which the information about the backbone can flow to the acquirer. First, joint quality assurance activities and a growing technical knowledge help the acquirer

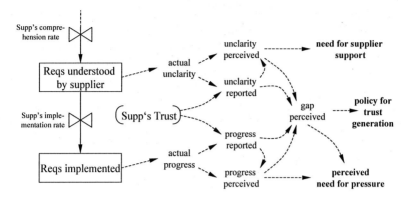

Figure 7.7.: Perceiving and reacting to the backbone's status

to see for himself how the supplier is doing; this is expressed through the "perceived"-variables. Second, the acquirer gets the supplier's reports about the status where the quality of these reports depend on the mutual trust. These two information sources form the acquirer's view on the unclarity of the requirements, on the progress in implementation, and even on the gap of the supplier's reports and the (perceived) reality. Hereupon, he can take appropriate action, like adapting task levels for supporting the supplier, increasing pressure or changing policy in order to enhance mutual trust.

This part of the model is a nice illustration of the increase in complexity due to the "reported"-variables as a further source of "subjectiveness" in addition to the "perceived"-variables. Although figure 7.7 shows only a part of the causal relationships associated with these variables, it should give a taste of their deep enmeshment in the model's causal web.

7.4.6. Acquirer's Knowledge Depletion

The explicit representation of "knowledge" is of minor importance in the system dynamics modeling of software *development* processes. Since the project's staff works for itself in all relevant technical matters, the technological expertise is "automatically" available. Knowledge is solely modeled implicitly through the differentiation of the staff in newly hired workforce and experienced workforce.

Knowledge has been modeled by work of McCray and Clark [52] on understanding outsourcing through System Dynamics; in fact, "knowledge" is among their main gauges to measure the success of an outsourcing strategy. They argue that the reduction of core competencies – and the acquirer always runs the risk of loosing them – has impacts on the strategic stance of the firms, since this makes it less capable of responding to its dynamic environment in a timely fashion. In a one-project view, as in our case, a representation of "knowledge" is also important, since it has a main influence on the effectiveness of the acquirer's monitoring and controlling activities. There are mainly two differences, however. In modeling software acquisition projects the representation of "knowledge" is just a means to an end and *not* a main indicator for project success. And furthermore, whereas McCray and Clark differ between separate knowledge bases for know-how in deployment, which has – amongst other things – impacts on the firm's application demand and know-how in internal development, we utilize solely one kind of knowledge, namely "technological knowledge". Both differences result from the fact that our focus is not on a firm's long-term development and future strategic market position. We are rather interested in factors that make *one* project successful or fail respectively.

Though the acquirer could attain know-how through special training courses, we solely care about knowledge obtained through interaction with the supplier especially through common quality assurance activities. This is by far the most relevant source of the acquirer's understanding because of its direct reference to the supplier's specific problems concerning technology and requirements realization. The corresponding part of the system dynamics model is shown in figure 7.8.

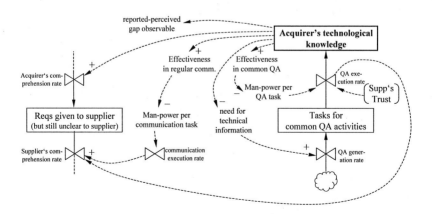

Figure 7.8.: Influences of acquirer's knowledge

Gaining knowledge is costly: the common quality assurance tasks require lots of manpower, and their performance can be difficult, particularly if there is a lack of mutual trust, which significantly hampers joint activities. On the other hand, a high level of the acquirer's understanding has significant positive impacts on an acquisition project:

- The most relevant project-supporting effect is an increase in the backbone's throughput or, in other words, an increase in the project's effectiveness: a high level of knowledge entails a rise in the acquirer's comprehension rate, and due to a growing efficiency in regular communication between acquirer and supplier, it may even indirectly have strengthening effects on the supplier's comprehension rate.

- When the acquirer's knowledge grows, he gains ability in perceiving gaps between the usually over-optimistic supplier's reports and the backbone's actual situation, and consequently he can take more appropriate action.

We can observe a positive (i.e. reinforcing) feedback loop through the fact that the higher the acquirer's level of knowledge gets, the more effective joint activities get, which in turn leads to a rise in the level in knowledge. Thus, gaining knowledge might become easier in the course of the project.

We proceeded deductively: we used the representation of "knowledge" in software development models and in IT outsourcing models as a basis for the treatment in this section.

7.4.7. Pressure and Supplier's Trust

This design section is the most hypothetical; all others refer – either through analogy or through antagonism and contrast – to (parts of) well-established system dynamics models of software development or outsourcing processes respectively. As regards modeling "trust" and "pressure", there are no apposite parts in corresponding software process models. Furthermore, "trust" and "pressure" are highly subjective and hardly measurable factors. However, they need to be represented, since one of our problems deals with them, namely problem 3 mentioned in section 7.1, and – even more important – they are obviously significant determinants of the efficacy (or lack thereof) of software acquisition projects. As for modeling subjective factors, Richardson and Pugh note:

"The modeler will probably always lack hard data for subjective concepts, such as pressure that results from being behind schedule, and yet they may be critically important to the behavior of a system. The intuitions of those closest to the problem will provide reliable dynamic views of such phenomena." [66], page 50

Nevertheless we try to justify each design decision as good as possible based on common sense.

Pressure can be solely applied through interaction with the supplier, and it cannot be treated separately from task performance. We therefore do not represent "pressure" as a separate object or level variable, but as a pressure portion in task performance rates using – as shown in figure 7.9 – an auxiliary variable called "%pressure".

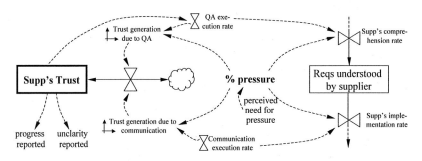

Figure 7.9.: Trust versus pressure in system dynamics notation

Applying pressure positively impacts the backbone's throughput: it increases the supplier's implementation rate and slight pressure might even strengthen the supplier's comprehension rate, since it restrains the supplier from being inattentive. However, the application of pressure is tightly coupled with the supplier's attitude towards the project and the acquirer; in lack of a better name, we call this attitude "Supplier's Trust", but we should keep in mind that it also comprises the supplier's motivation, confidence, and general mindset towards the project. A high portion of pressure in joint quality assurance activities lowers the trust level, and too much pressure in pure communication tasks might even be more harmful due to the lesser personal point of contact; these details are coded in the table functions "Trust generation due to QA" and "Trust generation due to Communication". A low trust level can be the most relevant factor for the failure of a software acquisition project. It hampers joint activities and deters the supplier to report (or, at least, to report the *actual* situation of) the project's state; this in turn falsifies the acquirer's most important gauge for project success, which is the basis for many actions.

7.4.8. The Complete Framework at a Glance

Figure 7.10 shows an outline of the complete system dynamics framework which points out, what the framework fractions cannot show: the "big" feedback loops: the perception of the backbone . . .

- . . . influences the generation and therefore the execution rate of the tasks for common quality assurance activities, and this, in turn, influences the throughput of the backbone. The backbone again determines the perception of the backbone and the feedback loop closes.

- . . . indirectly influences through respective actions the technological knowledge of the acquirer, which influences the throughput of the backbone. The backbone again determines the perception of the backbone and the feedback loop closes.

- . . . influences the pressure applied on the supplier. The pressure influences . . .

  - . . . the backbone's throughput and this again influences the perception of the backbone.

  - . . . the supplier's trust level; this influences the deviation of the supplier's reports from the reality and thus determines the perception of the backbone.

7.5. Integrative Models

We seek to develop *integrative* system dynamics models of software acquisition projects; *integrative* is meant in the sense of Abdel-Hamid and Madnick [1] – these models should incorporate *all* relevant aspects influencing the dynamics of a project.

The framework obviously focuses only on acquisition specific aspects of a project, and the question arises, if the scope determined by the framework suffices to model all relevant aspects of an acquisition project. After shortly presenting the scope of Abdel-Hamid and Madnick's model, presented in the

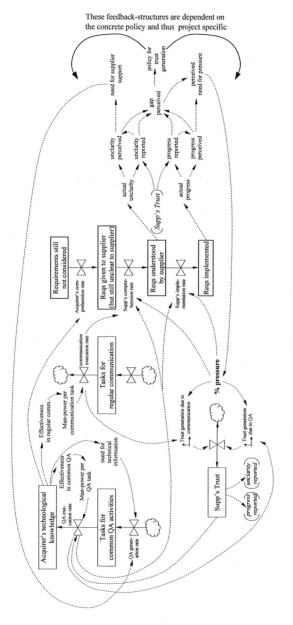

Figure 7.10.:: The complete model framework.

form of a subsystem structure, this section treats the question if a similar subdivision of system dynamics models of the software acquisition process is necessary, and, if the answer is "yes", how (or actually if) this fact influences the structure of the framework.

Actually, we already have a subdivision of emerging acquisition models through our treatment of the framework design in section 7.4; it results in the subsectors "Backbone", "Tasks", "Perceiving and reacting to the backbone's status", "Knowledge depletion", and "Pressure & Trust". Abdel-Hamid and Madnick's division shown in figure 7.11(a), however, is more coarse and hardly comparable to this structure. Through creating a basis for a direct comparison to the subsystem structure of Abdel-Hamid and Madnick's model, we hope to find gaps.

7.5.1. Subsystem Structures

Abdel Hamid and Madnick's model of the software development process integrates the aspects "Human resource management", "Controlling", "Planning", and "Software production"; figure 7.11(a) shows the respective subdivision of the model in subsystems.

As aforementioned, we want to find possible gaps in the framework through an attempt to form a respective structure for software acquisition models: planning and controlling are relevant aspects for every project, and so we can safely adopt the division in a "Planning" and a "Controlling" subsystem. "Supplier monitoring and controlling" is analogous to the "Software production" subsystem (cf. figure 7.11(a)) of the software development model in the following two respects: it is the subsystem which models the operative tasks of the project's staff, and it is the subsystem which comprises the domain specific aspects of the respective project. We thus get a comparable subsystem structure for the acquisition case, if we replace the "Software development" subsystem by the subsystem named "Supplier monitoring and controlling"; figure 7.11(b) shows the respective graph.

Though the subsystems are nearly identical, the labels of the edges connecting the subsystems greatly differ from the subsystem structure of software development models. This reflects one fundamental difference in the acquisition case: on the acquirer side, there is no predefined set of tasks which have to be performed in order to close the project; the tasks rather emerge in the course of the project. The acquirer is solely able to perform short term planning of the staff's tasks, and there is no such thing like "effort remaining" in the acquisition case. This short term view makes the "Controlling" and "Planning" subsystems simpler than the respective subsystems in

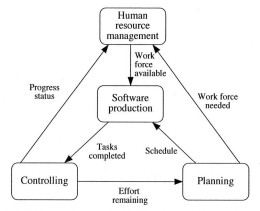

(a) Subsystems in Abdel-Hamid and Madnick's model [1]

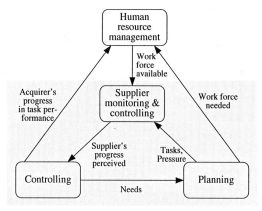

(b) A respective subsystem structure for the software acquisition case. The marked part is covered by the framework.

Figure 7.11.: Subsystem structure of Abdel-Hamid and Madnick's model compared to the subsystem structure of the acquisition framework

the software development model. Like in the software development case, the "Controlling" subsystem receives the backbone's status, but the difference is that – due to the aforementioned reason – a kind of "remaining effort" cannot be deduced; the "Controlling" subsystem rather issues a bundle of needs, and the "Planning" subsystem reacts accordingly through creating tasks and applying pressure.

Clearly, the framework covers the highly interweaved subsystems "Supplier monitoring and controlling", "Controlling", and "Planning". However, a "Human resource management" subsystem is missing for our emerging models to be integrative in the sense of Abdel-Hamid and Madnick. And in fact, in contrast to the "Controlling" and "Planning" subsystems, the "Human resource management" can be properly treated separately; its cohesion is adequately high, and its coupling with the framework is low enough to do this.

7.5.2. A Human Resource Management Subsystem

We already mentioned in the last section that, compared to the software development process, man-power allocation in software acquisition projects differs in one crucial aspect: the number of man-days remaining at a given point in time is not assessable in the same way. In software acquisition projects there, is no predefined set of tasks to be performed; the tasks rather emerge in the course of the project. Therefore, the allocation of man-power is solely oriented towards the tasks which are currently in the queue to be performed. Figure 7.12 shows the human resource management sector of an acquisition project as a supplement to the material presented in section 7.4. The marked part shows where it differs from the corresponding subsystem of a development project's model.

The human resource management subsystem consists of two levels, namely the "Newly hired work force" level and the "Experienced work force" level. We differentiate between these two types of staff members, since newly hired project members pass through an orientation phase, during which they are less than fully effective. During the course of the project, newly hired project members become experienced; this is accounted for through the "material" flow from the "Newly hired work force" level to the "Experienced work force" level controlled by the "Assimilation rate". The "Hiring rate", the "Quit rate", and the transfer rates allow to represent the fluctuation of project members.

Central in this subsystem is the variable "Work force level needed". There are two factors through which it is determined: first, the number of tasks

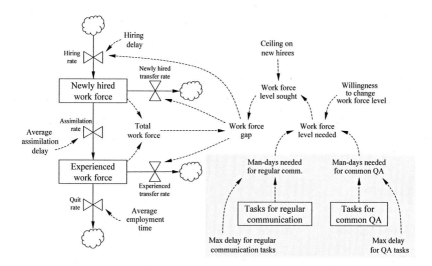

Figure 7.12.: The human resource management subsystem in an instantiation of the framework.

which are currently in the levels "Tasks for regular communication" and "Tasks for common quality assurance" (cf. section 7.4.4), and, second, the variables "Max delay for regular communication tasks" and "Max delay for QA tasks", specifying the maximal time spans during which the respective tasks should be executed – there are several reasons to limit the time during which the tasks have to be executed: for instance, planned activities simply get out of date after a certain period of time. There is a certain number of project members needed in order to execute all tasks during the respective maximal time spans given; the value of the variable "Work force level needed" is determined as the minimal such number.

The work force level the acquirer actually strives for is calculated in the variable "Work force level sought". It additionally accounts for two factors:

1. The "Willingness to change work force level" variable: the acquirer's willingness gets lower at the project end, typically when the time newly hired project members need to get oriented exceeds the project time remaining, i.e. when hiring new people gets ineffective.

2. The "Ceiling on new hires" variable: newly hired project members need training in order to get oriented, and part of this training is

performed through experienced project members. The ceiling should prevent that too much work force of the experienced staff is "wasted" through training newly hired staff members.

The work force gap which has to be closed is calculated through the variable "Work force level sought" minus the current total work force. This gap influences the hiring rate and the transfer rates of the existing work force; through adapting these rates, the acquirer seeks to close the work force gap.

7.6. The Universality of the Framework

We surely cannot exclude the possibility that reasonable models of software acquisition projects can be built which have substantially different structures than those provided by this framework. We claim, however, that all conceivable software acquisition project types can be sensibly modeled on the basis of this framework; more precisely, valid models (cf. section 7.7 and 8.6) of all conceivable software acquisition project types[3] can be built through extending the framework's system dynamics structures; the framework can be adapted to any given project scenario through extension. This claim can hardly be proved through a formal treatment; however, the following (and the concrete instantiating treated in section 8) should yield strong hints that this claim is valid.

Section 7.6.1 shows the backbone's adaptability; different project scenarios are listed and respective enhancements of the backbone are proposed. Section 7.6.2 treats the adaptability of the remaining framework components.

7.6.1. Backbone Adaptions

The backbone, which models the pass of requirements from the acquirer to the supplier, is the central part of the framework, and it also plays the central role in instantiating the framework. Therefore, the greatest part of this section treats the universality and adaptability of the backbone. Clearly, we can solely argue through examples, and we cannot provide an exhaustive treatment of project types, but the following examples of different project scenarios and respective backbone adaptions and/or extensions should indicate the backbone's adaptability.

---

[3]Note, that it is hardly possible to define the set of *all* software acquisition project types and scenarios. This contributes to the fact that it is impossible to formally prove our claim. However, a list of some project types is presented in section 7.6.1

- Projects in which a great portion of the requirements are established in advance: the backbone levels "Reqs given to supplier" and "Reqs understood by supplier" are initialized with adequately high values representing the requirements which are clear in advance.

- Projects in which the personnel of the supplier works closely with the acquirer personnel (e.g. sharing office space): the "Supplier's comprehension rate" should be set to a high value.

- Projects in which the acquirer is at a higher maturity level than the supplier (or vice versa): this is modeled through a steadily high "Acquirer's comprehension rate" and a volatile "Supplier's implementation rate".

- Projects in which the acquirer also tests himself; this is often the case where safety-critical software is acquired like for instance in the automotive environment.

In contrast to the aforementioned project scenarios, which could be represented through choosing the appropriate quantities for framework variables, a structural adaption of the framework is needed here. The acquirer's tests can be modeled through an additional level in the backbone indicating the requirements which are tested by the acquirer; then, the level indicating the implemented requirements has an outflow (controlled by a testing rate) into the level indicating the tested requirements. This is shown in figure 7.13.

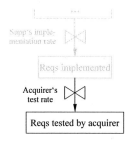

Figure 7.13.: A structural extension of the backbone needed to model software tests carried out on the acquirer's side.

7.6.2. Other Structural Adaptions

The description of other possible framework adaptions is shorter. We confine ourselves to describing *structural* refinements of the framework. However we should have in mind that the framework instantiation process comprises both, structural refinements *and* quantifications of framework elements.

The following table shows typical refinements which have to be made during the instantiation process. The first column shows framework parts which are actually essential parts for all instantiations, i.e. for all respective system dynamics models of software acquisition projects. The second column names the locations in the respective framework part which could be extended; the third column provides respective examples.

Must-Have	Refinements	Examples
"Progress" and "Unclarity" have to be represented as indicators of the earned value. There has to be an actual, a perceived, and a reported version of each "earned value".	In addition to "progress" and "unclarity", it is possible to represent other indicators of the earned value.	Acquirer's satisfaction, supplier's satisfaction, system's feasability, ...
Knowledge and its influence on effectiveness and monitoring and controlling capabilities have to be represented; there has to be an inflow from the "Tasks for common QA activities"-level into the knowledge level.	In addition to the inflow from the "Tasks for common QA activities"-level, it is possible to model other inflows.	A high trust could increase knowledge. Furthermore, the possibility of staff training and its influence on knowledge could be modeled.

The supplier's general mindset towards the project has to be represented through a level variable called "Trust". The task execution rates influence its inflow and outflow.	Additional model elements could influence the inflow and outflow of the "Trust" level.	The acquirer's knowledge could additionally influence the trust level; a high knowledge level could be daunting to the supplier which might rise the "Trust" level.
The pressure that the acquirer applies on the supplier has to be modeled through an auxiliary variable "%pressure" – a pressure portion.	Additional model elements could influence the pressure.	"Need for mututal trust", "Need for rigidity", etc.
At least two kinds of tasks, representing regular communication with the supplier and common quality assurance tasks, have to be represented as level variables.	The framework focuses on supplier monitoring and controlling tasks; however, task types representing other aspects of acquisition projects might be modeled. The modeling of the existing two task types in the framework should serve as a template for this.	"Tasks for testing", "Tasks for assessments / process audits", "Tasks for internal project management", ...

7.7. Validity of the Framework

We did not invent any novel modeling principles in designing the framework; we used solely existing principles and structures. This is ensured through the deductive proceeding in designing the framework structures. So, it is safe to say that we used valid methods and structures in the framework design – at least with respect to existing modeling projects on which the deductive design is based, namely the model of software development projects by Abdel-Hamid and Madnick [1], and the model of outsourcing information systems by McCray and Clark [52].

The question of the validity of the framework itself is more difficult. In order to judge its validity, we have to make aware the actual modeling goals; they provide the gauge through that we can assess the model's validity. It is safe to say that we showed the validity of the framework if we can show that the framework fulfils its goals.

1. The framework should be universal, i.e. it should be applicable on any acquisition project scenario: section 7.6 gives indicators that the framework actually is adequately universal.

2. The instantiation of the framework should yield *valid* system dynamics models of software acquisition projects: section 8.6 examines the validity of one specific framework instance.

Note, however, that the validation of a model is not a one-time activity which takes place after the model is built and before it is used; validation is always a process.

7.8. Concluding Remarks

We basically face two scientific camps in informatics. One camp seeks to approach problems on a formal mathematical basis – members are, for instance, the domains complexity theory, software construction through formal methods, and computational reasoning; claims can be objectively proved and are not challengeable (whereas their applicability to real-world problems sometimes *is* challengeable). The other camp seeks to approach problems on an empirical basis and through common sense – members are most branches of software engineering and software process research. Claims can hardly be proved but rather have to be justified empirically or, more formally, through statistical data and statistical analysis. Research in the field of software process simulation through System Dynamics is positioned *between* these two camps: it is based on claims and dynamic hypotheses, which can, in fact, hardly be proved – specially for software acquisition projects, there is hardly any data for real-world projects available; these hypotheses, however, are structured through System Dynamics, which has a formal mathematical basis, namely a set of interconnected differential equations. Between the informal hypotheses and the formal mathematical basis of system dynamics models lies the modeling process; the formality of this process determines the positioning of the whole modeling project with respect to the above mentioned scientific camps. Through the development of a framework and through the deductive approach employed in the design of the framework, we seek to shift this modeling project's research strategy more towards the first camp.

We want to simulate software acquisition projects through System Dynamics, and we have to start from the very beginning, since software acquisition is an unexplored domain in the system dynamics modeling literature. From a naive point of view, it might seem straightforward that the only thing to do is to generate specific models for software acquisition projects; a scientific approach, however, suggests – as a reasonable first step – abstraction. We abstract from specific acquisition models, and we first focus on common structures of all such models.

Basing the design on the experiences of one person, namely the author's experiences in consulting software acquisition projects, is not sufficient to yield a scientifically sound and unchallengeable fundament for system dynamics models. Therefore, we do not begin from scratch with the design of common acquisition structures; we start at existing achievements in neighboring domains, namely the system dynamics modeling of software development and the system dynamics modeling of information systems outsourcing. From these firm starting points, we can approach our goals of capturing the common structures in a safer way.

The main part of this chapter tries to answer the question, what the common causal structures of acquisition models are. But important questions remain:

- *Validity*: Is the framework valid with respect to its purposes? Does it indeed capture the essential structures of acquisition models, and does it enable a modeler to design valid system dynamics models of the acquisition process?

- *Universality*: Is the framework adaptable enough? Is it capable of covering a sufficiently wide range of software acquisition project types?

Surely, this chapter alone cannot safely show that the framework has indeed the degree of universality that we claim and that we require. Section 7.6 gives hints but no proofs. The same is true for the framework's validity: section 7.7 gives hints on its validity, and we will get stronger hints through subsequent instantiations of the framework, but this chapter cannot present proofs for the validity. Furthermore, one should realize that showing the universality and validity of this system dynamics framework is a continuous process; it is not a one-time activity. The framework will be applied to many different kinds of software acquisition project scenarios in the near future. This process will deliver stronger conclusions with respect to the universality and – partly related with this – validity of the framework.

Chapter 8

A System Dynamics Model of Software Acquisition Projects

In this chapter, we describe an executable system dynamics model of a software acquisition project. The model is an instantiation of the framework described in section 7.4. On the basis of a concrete software acquisition project described in section 8.1, the framework is concretized in two aspects:

1. The actual structure of the framework is adapted to the case study through refinements. Some variables are subdivided, auxiliary variables are added and additional functional dependencies are added. Section 8.2 describes these refinements.

2. All level, rate, and auxiliary variables are quantified. Section 8.3 explains the quantification of the most important model variables and justifies them as far as possible.

This framework implementation has been realized as a Vensim simulation model which is presented in section 8.4.

The rest of this chapter is also closely related to the chapter 7: not until this chapter, we can test if the requirements which were incorporated in the design of the framework are actually fulfilled. Based on the modeling "problems" discussed in section 7.1, outputs of this system dynamics model are presented, and their implications on modeling "problems" (i.e. the questions we want to answer through simulation) are analyzed in section 8.5. Section 8.6 discusses the validity of the system dynamics model through answering the question if the actual modeling purposes are achieved and through analyzing if the model is capable of reproducing the reference behavior modes (which are stated in section 7.1). Section 8.7 concludes this chapter.

8.1. The Case Study

A real-world acquisition project in the automotive environment serves as a case study for using the framework. Embedded software for cars is procured and the project has an evolutionary touch. For some software modules, there exists a great number of different versions due to the many different car models; this makes this kind of automotive software acquisition particularly complex.

There is one approved standard supplier who already cooperated in many prior similar projects of this department and the level of mutual trust between acquirer and supplier is high. In this respect, the most important adaption to the framework is to give the "Supp's Trust"-level (cf. figure 7.9) a high initial value and to make it more resistant to change (e.g. through respective design of the table functions "Trust generation due to QA" and "Trust generation due to communication"). Furthermore, the "Supp's comprehension rate" is chosen higher than in projects with no standard supplier. The supplier's job in this project is to advance existing software and to adopt it for adherence to changing standards; the basic set of requirements is similar to those of prior projects, so we have the aforementioned case (cf. section 7.6 about the universality of the framework) of a project in which a great portion of the requirements is clear in advance. The backbone is adapted accordingly, i.e. the backbone levels "Requirements still not considered", "Requirements given to supplier", and "Requirements understood by supplier" are set to a high initial value.

Correctness in embedded automotive software is crucial. Thus, in addition to testing activities on the supplier side (which are not represented in our model – our focus is on the acquisition project itself) there are, in this concrete project, also testing activities on the acquirer's side.

We tailor the system dynamics framework to this case study. The next two sections describe the corresponding instantiation of the framework.

8.2. Structural Refinements

The framework as described in the last chapter forms only the skeleton of system dynamics models. It has to be both structurally refined and the relationships between the variables have to be concretized. This section describes the most important structural refinements of the framework.

The subdivision in sections which we use here is similar to the subdivision we used to present the system dynamics framework in the previous chapter. After discussing possible extensions to model testing activities on the acquirer's side, we describe extensions of the backbone in section 8.2.2, extensions of the framework's part modeling the backbone's perception in section 8.2.3, extensions in the representation of the tasks in section 8.2.4 and, finally, extensions of the framework's part modeling the pressure in section 8.2.5. However, there is no section about the refinement of the knowledge depletion part of the framework; hardly any extensions were necessary there.

The figures illustrating the refinements, namely figures 8.1, 8.2, 8.3, and 8.4, show the parts defined by the framework in gray. The new variables and flows are bold.

8.2.1. Acquirer's Testing Activities

Section 7.6 suggests that software acquisition projects in which the acquirer also performs tests (in addition to the supplier tests) might, but need not, be modelled through extending the backbone with an additional level "Requirements tested by acquirer", like it is shown in figure 7.13. In the case of this concrete case study, we choose *not* to follow this suggestion, for the following reasons:

- The project (i.e. the acquirer project) for which this system dynamics model was originally developed focuses on problems regarding the interaction with the supplier; the project members see minor problems in their testing activities. We would surely have to rethink the decision *not* to model the acquirer's testing activities, if the project members were more interested in problems concerning their testing processes.

- It turned out that the system boundary can easily be drawn in such a way that the acquirer's testing activities are outside the system to be modeled. In our case, there are no feedback loops which couple these testing activities with the rest of the model. The internal view (cf. section 6.1) remains intact.

In other cases, there might well be feedback structures which couple the acquirer's testing activities with the rest of the model, and thus making it impossible to omit the representation of testing without violating the internal view on the acquisition project. An example could be a strong influence of the acquirer's technological knowledge on the testing activities and an influence of the testing results on the trust on the supplier and the need for controlling and monitoring the supplier; this would form feedback structures connecting the testing to the rest of the model and the model would influence the testing, and the testing, again, would influence the model.

In the case of this specific case study, however, we see just a minor influence of the acquirer's technological know-how, which he gains during the course of the project, and the performance of his own testing activities; since this project has an evolutionary touch, the acquirer already has (from prior stages of the evolution) a great portion of the technological know-how, needed for testing, in advance.

8.2.2. Backbone

The rate variables that control the requirements' flow underly complex influences and these three rate variables are thus refined in the framework's implementation:

- The "Acquirer's comprehension rate" is refined with the auxiliary variable "littleness factor". It accommodates the fact that the smaller the number of unconsidered requirements is, the more difficult it gets for the acquirer to reveal unconsidered requirements.

- A factor "Comprehension from Tasks" is added to the supplier's comprehension rate. It accommodates the fact the that communication between the acquirer and the supplier improves the supplier's ability to comprehend the requirements.

- We further add the variables "Basic comprehension rate" and "Basic implementation rate" modeling the basic capabilities of the supplier.

- The "Supp's implementation rate" is refined with the auxiliary factor "unclarity factor". It accommodates the fact that the more requirements are not clear to the supplier, the more errors, slack and rework has to be done, i.e. the smaller the actual implementation rate is.

An overview on these refinements can be found in figure 8.1.

8.2.3. Perceiving the Backbone's Status

We add the auxiliary variable "reported ratio" which calculates to what ratio the supplier's reports and to what ratio the reality determines what the acquirer perceives.

The auxiliary variable "reported time factor" determines the supplier's possibilities to let his reports diverge from reality.

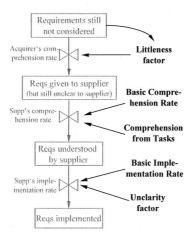

Figure 8.1.: Structural refinement of the backbone

8.2.4. Tasks

The tasks require minor refinements. We solely add an auxiliary variable "Willingness for common QA". This variable expresses the extent to which the acquirer is actually willing the plan for new common quality assurance activities. The intention for inventing this new factor is the fact that planing and executing common quality assurance activities takes much time, and it hardly makes sense to plan for new QA activities when the project is nearly finished.

Figure 8.3 shows this extension. Since there are no structural extensions corresponding to the level variable "Tasks for regular communication", figure 8.3 shows only the part of the framework representing the tasks for common quality assurance.

8.2.5. Pressure

We refine the part of the framework modeling the influence of pressure on the supplier's comprehension rate and the supplier's implementation rate. The framework solely prescribes – as shown in figure 7.9 on page 123 – that the factor "%pressure" together with the rate variable "QA execution rate" influences the supplier's comprehension rate and, analogously, that the factor "%pressure" together with the rate variable "Communication execution rate"

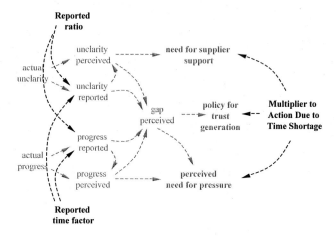

Figure 8.2.: Structural refinement in modeling the backbone's perception.

Figure 8.3.: Structural refinement in modeling the tasks.

influences the supplier's implementation rate.

In our case, these influences are complex, and we therefore refine this prescription through introducing additional intermediate factors, which are shown in figure 8.4: the variable "QA pressure" represents the level of pressure applied through common quality assurance, and the variable "Communication pressure" represents the level of pressure applied through regular communication activities. Introducing these factors is important since this allows to conveniently model different assumptions about the intensity of pressure application through common quality assurance and through regular communication, respectively. The factors "QA pressure" and "communication pressure" effect the supplier's comprehension rate and the supplier's

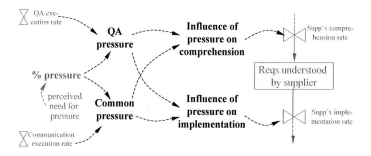

Figure 8.4.: Structural refinement in modeling pressure.

implementation rate to different fractions. We model this fact through the variables "Influence of pressure on comprehension" and "Influence of pressure on implementation". Section 8.3.5 describes the respective quantification of all these factors.

8.3. Quantifications

The quantification of the most important factors of the executable model is described in this section. The quantitative form of these factors is justified as far as possible. Note, however, that this section is full of hypotheses, sometimes even arguable assumptions. There are still many unclarities about causal relationships in an acquisition project, and we face the common problem of missing data of real-world acquisition projects. These hypotheses are therefore inevitable to build a complete *quantitative* model. The fact that we are dealing with many assumptions should not be seen as any kind of drawback in this model; it rather is the usual case in nearly all system dynamics models of human systems. In fact, we actually *want* to use System Dynamics to model hypotheses (cf. our modeling purposes treated in section 6.4).

The subdivision we use to present the variables' quantification is similar to the subdivision we used to present the system dynamics framework in the previous chapter; so, the variables' quantification is divided into variables used to model the perception of the backbone (section 8.3.1), variables used to model reactions to the backbone's status (section 8.3.2), variables used to model knowledge depletion (section 8.3.3), variables used to model the supplier's trust (section 8.3.4), variables used to model pressure application (section 8.3.5), variables used to model tasks (section 8.3.6), variables used to model manpower allocation (section 8.3.7), and variables used to model the backbone (section 8.3.8).

The description of each variable quantification is structured as follows: first, the variable name is presented followed by a short description of the variable's meaning. Second, we present the formula (together with a possibly lengthy explanation of the formula) specifying how the variable is calculated. We additionally list which variables are influenced, and, finally, we state the value range of the variable. Some variables have fixed ranges, some variables have flexible ranges, i.e. the ranges depend on the value of other system variables; we indicate flexible ranges with an additional "∼". For instance, $[0, \sim2]$ means that the respective variable is located in the interval $[0, 2]$ provided that all other variables are ranged in "reasonable" intervals, or, in other words, the respective variable is located in $[0, 2]$ in all simulation runs representing realistic scenarios.

8.3.1. Perceiving the Backbone's Status

For many variables in the part of the model describing the perception of the backbone, there exist two versions:

1. the actual, perceived, reported status of the *progress* plus the perceived gap of the reported and perceived status of the progress

2. and, accordingly, the actual, perceived, reported status of the *unclarity* on the supplier side and the perceived gap of the reported and perceived status of the unclarity.

Apart from the *actual* unclarity and *actual* progress the quantification of the "progress"- and the respective "unclarity"-versions is nearly identical, and, thus, we treat solely the "progress"-versions of the variables in this section.

- **Actual progress**

  Determines the fraction of requirements which are implemented so far.

  Formula: $\dfrac{\texttt{Reqs implemented}}{\texttt{Total Requirements}}$

  Influences: progress perceived, progress reported
  Value range: $[0, 1]$

- Actual unclarity

  The fraction of the requirements which are neither understood by the supplier (Reqs understood by supplier) nor implemented (Reqs implemented).

  Formula: $1 - \dfrac{\texttt{Reqs understood by Supplier+Reqs implemented}}{\texttt{Total Requirements}}$

  Influences: unclarity perceived, unclarity reported

  Value range: $[0, 1]$

- reported time factor

  Determines the supplier's possibilities to let his reports diverge from reality.

  Formula: Lookup(time) with table function shown in figure 8.5.

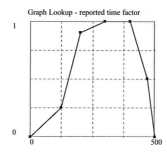

Figure 8.5.: Table function used in reported time factor

  Diverges of the supplier's reports from reality can happen deliberately, when the supplier wants to avoid any kind of trouble in the short run, or not deliberately through an inability to assess the project's progress and status realistically – most often it is a mixture of both factors. Complete ignorance on the acquirer's side provided, a reported time factor of 1 indicates that the supplier could pervert the facts arbitrarily (but need not – whether he lets his reports really diverge from reality depends on a bunch of other factors) without it being noticed by the acquirer; a value of zero indicates, accordingly, that the supplier has to stick to reality in his reports and, in fact, is also able to do this.

At the beginning and at the very end, the supplier cannot deviate from reality in his reports since this would be too obvious for the other side. Therefore, during these periods, the `reported time factor` is zero or near zero. We know from experience that "lies" at an early phase of the project are even more obvious than around the end of the project – it is often possible to conceal the truth even on the verge of the project's closure; unrealistically optimistic reports on the first quarter of the project, on the other hand, often seem suspicious to the acquirer. Therefore, the gradient of the curve is much smaller in the first quarter than in the last quarter. In the middle phase of the project, the supplier could "lie" unhamperedly (of course, however, under the unrealistic assumption that the acquirer is totally ignorant and does not take any counteractive actions).

Influences: `progress reported, unclarity reported`

Value range: $[0, 1]$

- `progress reported`

Determines the project's progress as reported from the supplier to the acquirer.

Formula: `actual progress` $+ (1 - $ `Trust ratio`$) *$
`reported time factor` $* (1 - $ `actual progress`$)$

It is assumed here that the progress reported is *always* greater than the actual progress, i.e. the supplier always tends towards glossing over – consciously or unconsciously – delays in progress and lacks in his understanding of the requirements. In determining the `progress reported`, a fraction of the value "1 − actual-progress" is added to the actual progress. Two factors influence the amount of this fraction:

- The supplier's trust level
- The phase in which the project currently is which is represented through the `reported time factor`. It determines how much the supplier's reports may deviate from reality.

The factor `unclarity reported` is determined analogously.

Influences: `progress perceived, progress gap`

Value range: $[0, 1]$

- reported ratio

Determines the ratio which the supplier's reports contribute to the acquirer's view on the project state.

Formula: Lookup(QA execution rate) with table function shown in figure 8.6.

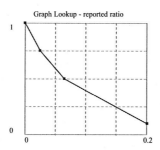

Figure 8.6.: Table function used in reported ratio

Assume that there are no common quality assurance activities; then the supplier can hardly perceive differently from the supplier's reports due to the lack of direct information. In this case, the reported fraction is 1. The acquirer starts to see more than he is reported, when there are common quality assurance activities; for this, the curve has a higher gradient at the beginning. Even when there are very many common quality assurance activities, a vestige of insecurity cannot be eliminated; the curve thus flattens at greater execution rates and never reaches zero.

Influences: actual reported ratio

Value range: $[0, 1]$

- actual reported ratio

Similar than reported ratio but the acquirer's technological knowledge is accounted for.

Formula: reported ratio $* (1 -$ Acq's Technological Knowledge)
The acquirer gets insight through respective common quality activities, but he also needs the respective knowledge in order to be able to classify his impressions properly and to draw reasonable conclusions. So, the Technological Knowledge also plays

an important role in determining what part of reality the acquirer actually perceives. There are two perceivable possibilities to combine `reported ratio` and `Technological Knowledge`:

1. The arithmetic mean of the two factors.
2. The multiplication of the two factors.

Forming the arithmetic mean of the two factors would imply that the acquirer could be able to assess the project's progress at least partly even if he has absolutely no technological knowledge, or – vice versa – the acquirer can partly assess the project's progress even with no direct interaction with the supplier provided his technological know-how is good. This is not conform with reality, and we choose the second possibility to combine the two factors.

Influences: `progress perceived, unclarity perceived`

Value range: $[0, 1]$

- `progress perceived`

Determines the project's progress as perceived by the acquirer

Formula: `actual reported ratio * progress reported + (1 − actual reported ratio * progress perceived)`

The progress perceived by the acquirer is the weighted average of the "reported" and the "actual" progress. The respective weight is determined by the variable `actual reported ratio`. The case with `unclarity perceived` is analogous.

Influences: `unclarity gap, need for supplier support`

Value range: $[0, 1]$

- `Progress gap`

Denotes the gap between the reported and the perceived progress.

Formula: $\dfrac{|\texttt{progress reported–progress perceived}|}{\texttt{progress perceived}}$

This denotes the gap between the reported progress and the progress perceived by the acquirer (as the relative deviation from the perceived progress). The variable `unclarity gap` is determined analogously.

Influences: `Gap perceived`

Value range: $[0, \sim\!2]$

- Gap perceived

Determines the gap between reported and actual information as perceived by the acquirer.

Formula: $\dfrac{\texttt{Progress gap} + \texttt{Unclarity gap}}{2}$

The `Gap perceived` is simply the arithmetic mean of the `progress gap` and the `unclarity gap`. This denotes the common gap between the supplier's reports and the reality perceived by the acquirer. A huge gap is an important signal indicating threat for the acquirer: appropriate action is required in order to enhance the relationship with the supplier and/or (dependent on the policy in use) to monitor and control the supplier more effectively.

Influences: `Need for status information,`
`Need for technical information,`
`policy for trust generation`

Value range: $[0, \sim 2]$

8.3.2. Reacting to the Backbone's Status

- Need for techn know-how

Determines the need perceived by the acquirer to gather more technological knowledge.

Formula: $(1 - \texttt{Acq's technological Knowledge}) * \texttt{gap perceived}$

The gap between the reports of the supplier and the (assumed) reality is an indication for the acquirer to care about the enhancement of his technological know-how. The value of `gap perceived` is therefore a factor which influences `Need for techn know-how`. We assume that the acquirer has full insight in the state of his technological understanding (this is not self-evident; ignorance about the own ignorance is probably more common) and, thus, `Acq's techn know-how` is another factor which influences the variable `Need for techn know-how`.

The question remains how to combine these two factors in determining the `Need for techn know-how`. We favor a multiplicative combination. A strong indication that this is a reasonable choice is the fact that both if `gap perceived` is near zero then `Need for techn know-how` should be near zero *and* if `Acq's techn know-how` is near zero then `Need for techn know-how` should also be near zero. The following consideration shows that these dependencies are reasonable: Suppose the acquirer knows about the gaps in is own knowledge. When the reports seem to be conform to reality (more concise: what he perceives as reality), there is no reasonable need for any action and particularly no need for acquiring more technological know-how. And vice versa, even if the reports do not seem to be conformant to reality at all, if the acquirer thinks his level of technological know-how is adequate (i.e. the factor $1 - $ `Acq's technological Knowledge` is zero or near zero), then there would be, of course, no perceived need for him to acquire more knowledge, and `Need for techn know-how` also should be zero or near zero.

Influences: `QA generation rate`

Value range: $[0, \sim\!1]$

- `Multiplier to action due to time shortage`

Determines the vehemence of the acquirer's reactions to perceived gaps.

Formula: Lookup(`time`) with table function shown in figure 8.7.

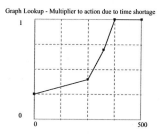

Figure 8.7.: Table function used in `Multiplier to action due to time shortage`

We assume that the acquirer might react as far as four times as vehement when time gets short and he has to worry about serious delays in the project schedule. During the first half of the project's course, the value grows slowly. In the third quarter, the curve rises steeply; things become urgent and the acquirer runs scared. In the last quarter of the project, the acquirer tries to do anything in his power to cope with the problems perceived.

This multiplier is used by all model variables denoting the need for action except by `Need for techn know-how`. This is due to the assumption that the acquirer knows that acquiring knowledge needs time, and that it is not reasonable to enforce this need near the closure of the project when the project runs the risk of getting late.

Influences: `Need for controlling and pressure,`
`Need for supplier support,` `Need for status information`

Value range: $[0.25, 1]$

- `Need for controlling and pressure`

Determines the need perceived by the acquirer to enforce controlling of and pressure on the supplier.

Formula: $\max(0, ($`target progress` $-$ `progress perceived`$))*$
`Multiplier to action due to time shortage`

A discrepancy between the planned progress, i.e. `target progress`, and the progress perceived by the acquirer, i.e. `progress perceived`, leads to the need of applying a higher amount of pressure and control on the supplier. How urgent this need is experienced by the acquirer further depends on the project's current phase (cf. `Multiplier to action due to time shortage`).

Influences: `comm generation rate,` `%pressure,`
`QA generation rate`

Value range: $[0, {\sim}1]$

- `Need for status information`

Determines the need perceived by the acquirer to demand more status information from the acquirer.

Formula: `gap perceived` $*$
`Multiplier to action due to time shortage`

The gap the acquirer perceives between the reported and the perceived information, i.e. `gap perceived`, directly translates into the need to ask for more detailed information about the project's status. How urgent this need is experienced by the acquirer further depends on the project's current phase (cf. `Multiplier to action due to time shortage`)

Influences: `comm generation rate` – in order to get solely status information, no costly common quality assurance activities need to be performed. Status information can be asked for – at least for the most part – through direct communication, for instance, telephone calls or management meetings.

Value range: $[0, \sim1]$

- `Need for supplier support`

Determines the need perceived by the acquirer to increase support for the supplier (in understanding and implementing requirements).

Formula: `unclarity perceived *`
          `Multiplier to action due to time shortage`

The support (e.g. support in understanding the requirements or support in explaining certain technical details in which the acquirer is better skilled than the supplier) which the acquirer wants to give to the supplier depends on the level of unclarity on the supplier side, or – more precisely – on what the acquirer perceives to be the unclarity on the supplier side. The level of support further depends on the urgency which results from the project's current phase and its risk for getting late; therefore, the perceived unclarity is multiplied with the factor `Multiplier to action due to time shortage`.

Influences: `comm generation rate`

Value range: $[0, \sim1]$

8.3.3. Knowledge Depletion

- `Acquirer's Technological Knowledge`

Denotes the technological know-how of the acquirer which improves the acquirer's ability to assess the actual state of the software developed by the supplier.

Formula: Lookup(`QA Tasks Performed`) with table function shown in figure 8.8.
The shape of this curve is dependent on the respective characteristics of the acquirer. The value for $x = 0$ depends on the technical know-how which the acquirer brings along to the project. In this

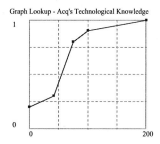

Figure 8.8.: Table function used in `Acquirer's Technological Knowledge`

case, we assume a quite low know-how at the beginning – approximately one fifth of what he is able to understand in the course of the project. At the project start, there is a missing knowledge basis (at least in our case) which implies that there is a relative low increase in knowledge and the curve rises slowly during the first common quality assurance activities; the curve's gradient raises when a solid knowledge basis is built up – i.e. the acquirer starts to learn more quickly. We assume a saturation from a certain amount of common quality assurance activities on; the acquirer knows enough to reasonably assess the project's situation, and further learning of technical details has less effects on his abilities.

Influences: `Effectiveness in QA activities,`
`effectiveness in regular comm,`
`Acquirer's comprehension rate, actual reported ratio,`
`Need for technical Know How`

Value range: $[0, 1]$

8.3.4. Trust

- `Trust generation due to QA`

  Models the influence of pressure (applied in combination with common quality assurance activities) on the supplier's trust.

  Formula: Lookup(`%pressure * QA execution rate`) with table function shown in figure 8.9.
  This models the influence of pressure (applied in combination with

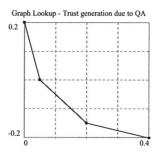

Figure 8.9.: Table function used in `Trust generation due to QA`

common quality assurance activities) on the supplier's trust in the acquirer and the supplier's general mindset towards the project (for the exact meaning of "trust" in this model, see section 7.4.7). Two things need to be explained here:

1. The question why we choose the *multiplication* as the combination of the factors `%pressure` and `QA execution rate` as input to the table function

2. The table function's shape.

Pressure can solely be applied through interaction with the supplier; pressure cannot be treated separately in this model. The %-sign already indicates the reasons for choosing the multiplication as a combination of the two factors: `%pressure` is the portion of pressure in the interaction with the supplier, and so `%pressure * QA execution rate` can be seen as the pressure applied to the supplier through common quality assurance activities.

Note that the table function shown in figure 8.9) whose x-axis is labeled with pressure applied through common QA activities, is quite hypothetical and in fact *has to be* hypothetical since it is hardly possible to collect data about pressure and trust levels and the respective influence of pressure on trust. Nevertheless, we describe the assumptions underlying the shape of this table function: it is reasonable that increasing pressure always entails decreasing trust, and therefore the table function should be monotonically decreasing. We further assume that low pressure makes more difference compared to high pressure than high pressure compared to very high pressure. Therefore, the shape of the curve should be convex.

Influences: Trust generation rate
Value range: $[-0.2, 0.2]$

- Trust generation due to Communication

Models the influence of communication on trust.

Formula: Lookup(%pressure * communication execution rate) with table function shown in figure 8.10.

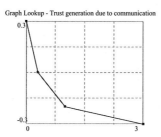

Graph Lookup - Trust generation due to communication

Figure 8.10.: Table function used in Trust generation due to Communication

The x-axis of the table function denotes the pressure applied to the supplier through regular communication between the acquirer and the supplier. The shape of the table function is similar to the shape of the table function used by the "Trust generation due to QA" variable, but its decrease is greater in the first half. The reason for this is that pressure applied through common quality activities may be better tolerated, since the acquirer productively works together with the supplier, whereas pressure applied through pure communication might appear patronizing. We assume that the supplier reacts more sensibly to this kind of pressure.

Influences: Trust generation rate
Value range: $[-0.3, 0.3]$

- Trust generation rate
Formula: Trust generation due to QA+
       Trust generation due to Communication

The general trust generation rate is simply the summation of the trust generation through common quality assurance activities and the trust generation through communication.

Influences: `Supplier's Trust`

Value range: $[-0.5, 0.5]$

8.3.5. Pressure and Its Influence on the Backbone's Throughput

- `%pressure`

  Denotes the pressure portion which the acquirer applies in interaction activities with the supplier.

  Formula: `Need for controlling and pressure * pressure policy`
  Note that this variable is exclusively used in combination with task execution rates. Pressure can be solely applied through interaction with the supplier and cannot act on the project dynamics apart.

  The need for controlling and pressure resulting from the perception of the backbones' status translates directly into the pressure which the acquirer seeks to apply. This may additionally be enforced or diluted, respectively, through the variable `pressure policy`. This factor makes it easy for the modeler to experiment with different pressure strategies.

  Influences: `QA pressure, Comm pressure`

  Value range: $[0, \sim 1]$

- `QA pressure`

  Denotes the pressure applied through quality assurance activities.

  Formula: `%pressure * QA execution rate * 70`
  The variable `%pressure` denotes the pressure *portion* of interactions with the supplier. So, the multiplication of the execution rate for common quality assurance activities with the pressure portion represents the pressure which is applied through common quality assurance tasks.

  The factor 70 calibrates its value for the interval $[0, 1]$.

  Influences: `influence of pressure on comprehension,`
  `influence of pressure on implementation`

  Value range: $[0, 1]$

- `Comm pressure`

  Denotes the pressure applied through regular communication.

Formula: `%pressure * Communication execution rate * 1.5`

The multiplication of the execution rate for regular communication with the pressure portion represents the pressure which is applied through regular communication.

The factor 1.5 calibrates its value for the interval $[0, 1]$

Influences: `influence of pressure on comprehension`, `influence of pressure on implementation`

Value range: $[0, 1]$

- `influence of pressure on comprehension`

Models the influence of pressure application on the supplier's comprehension rate.

Formula: $\text{Lookup}((2 * \texttt{QA pressure} + \texttt{Comm pressure})/3)$ with table function shown in figure 8.11.

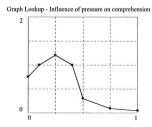

Graph Lookup - Influence of pressure on comprehension

Figure 8.11.: Table function used in `influence of pressure on comprehension`

The shape of this curve is very much dependent on the characteristics of the specific supplier, and even if the supplier is well-known this curve is always hypothetical. In our case, we suppose the following: if no pressure is applied through interactions with the supplier – this corresponds to an x-value of 0 – then the supplier's performance is a bit less than under ideal conditions, i.e. the y-value is a bit less than 1. Moderate pressure increases the supplier's performance. On the other hand, it is a truism that too much pressure harms productivity. Which amount can be considered as too much is very much dependent on the concrete person or group of persons. In our case, we assume that the pressure application of more than a third of the maximum possible pressure application is "too much" and the supplier looses abilities in comprehension when the amount of pressure exceeds this threshold.

There are two further assumptions underlying this curve:

- The limit of the maximum tolerable pressure by the supplier is associated with a *sudden* drop of the curve, i.e. the supplier reacts sensibly to too much pressure with a sudden drop in his ability to efficiently comprehend what the acquirer needs.
- Pressure applied through common quality assurance activities has a greater influence on the comprehension rate than pressure applied through regular communication. This is because, for the supplier to comprehend the requirements more efficiently, detailed explanation is needed which can more easily be provided through common quality assurance activities like common reviews or common risk management.

Influences: Supplier's comprehension rate

Value range: $[0.05, 1.2]$

- influence of pressure on implementation

Models the influence of pressure application on the supplier's implementation rate.

Formula: Lookup$((2 * \text{Comm pressure} + \text{QA pressure})/3)$ with table function shown in figure 8.12.

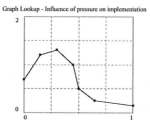

Graph Lookup - Influence of pressure on implementation

Figure 8.12.: Table function used in influence of pressure on implementation

The shape of this curve is – like the shape of the lookup function for influence of pressure on comprehension – very much dependent on the characteristics of the specific supplier, and even if the supplier is well-known this curve is always hypothetical.

If no pressure is applied through interactions with the supplier – this corresponds to an x-value of 0 – then the supplier's performance is a bit less than under ideal conditions, i.e. the y-value is a bit less than 1. Similar than in the case of pressure's influence on comprehension, moderate pressure increases the supplier's performance whereas too much pressure harms productivity. But we assume two differences to the respective table function for the influence of pressure on comprehension: first, the curve's decrease is shifted rightwards which means that the supplier's pressure tolerance is higher when he implements than when he comprehends – comprehension is a more intellectual and less mechanical activity than implementation, and thus comprehension is the more sensible task. Second, the curve's bottom is not as low as in the comprehension case, and this is again for the same reason - implementation is less sensible to disturbances like an excessive amount of pressure from the acquirer.

Influences: `Supp's implementation rate`

Value range: $[0.15, 1.3]$

8.3.6. Tasks

- `communication generation rate`

  Denotes the rate with which tasks for regular communication are generated by the management of the acquirer project.

  Formula: `Nominal communication generation rate *`
  `(Need for status information +`
  `Need for controlling and pressure +`
  `Need for supplier support)`

  There are three sources indicating the need for this kind of communication:

  - The need for status information: the easiest way to get more information about the status of the supplier's project is to plan for more "regular communication" activities, i.e. more communication via e-mail, telephone, or short direct meetings with the supplier.
  - The need for controlling and pressure: when the acquirer wants to have more control over the supplier's project then he increases – amongst other things like increasing pressure

or increasing common activities – the tasks for regular communication. One might expect both psychological effects, i.e. as the supplier notices that the acquirer "tightens the reins" he will hopefully be more conscientious about the project, and effects regarding the acquirer's knowledge about the project's status which makes the acquirer again more capable of controlling the supplier effectively.

– The need for supplier support: smaller unclarities and questions can be clarified through regular communication tasks, e.g. through e-mails or telephone calls.

The question remains how to combine them. Multiplication is surely not reasonable since this entails that a low value in just one of the above needs would imply an overall low communication rate. We rather use the summation of the three factors as a multiplier for the `Nominal communication generation rate`.

Influences: `Tasks for regular communication`

Value range: $[0, \sim2]$

- `communication execution rate`

Denotes the rate with which tasks for regular communication are executed by the staff of the acquirer project.

Formula: $\min($`Tasks for regular communication,`
$$\frac{\texttt{Man power for reg Comm}}{\texttt{actual Man-Days needed per comm task}})$$
The execution rate for regular communication tasks is dependent on the man power available for communication which is represented through the variable `Man power for reg communication`. Additionally, it is dependent on how effective the communication is. This is expressed through the variable `actual Man-Days needed per comm task` which is influenced by the acquirer's technological knowledge – the better the know-how, the more effective the communication.

Furthermore, the execution rate cannot be greater than the number of the current fixed tasks, and its amount is thus bounded by the value of the variable `Tasks for regular communication`.

Influences: `Comprehension from tasks,`
`Trust generation due to communication`

Value range: $[0, \sim3]$

- QA generation rate

Denotes the rate with which tasks for common quality assurance activities are generated by the management of the acquirer's project.

Formula: min(Maximum QA generation rate,
(Need for controlling and pressure +
Need for techn Know How) $* 0.2 *$
Willingness for common QA)

There are two sources indicating the need for common quality assurance:

– The need for controlling and pressure: one way to increase pressure and control over the supplier's project is to plan for more common quality assurance activities. Due to the direct (independent of the supplier's reports) source of information which the acquirer gets through common QA activities, he gains ability to control the supplier more adequately. Furthermore, light pressure in combination with the execution of common quality assurance tasks might be the most helpful way to "tighten the reins".

– The need for technical know-how: as justified in section 7.4.6, in our model, technological knowledge can be obtained solely through common quality assurance activities. So, planning for more common quality assurance tasks is the first choice when there is demand for acquiring more knowledge.

Planning for common quality assurance tasks makes less sense during the last phases of the project; this fact is modeled through the multiplication of the factor Willingness for common QA.

Influences: Tasks for common QA activities

Value range: $[0, \sim 0.2]$

- Willingness for common QA

Denotes the acquirer's willingness to plan for new quality assurance activities.

Formula: Lookup(time remaining) with table function shown in figure 8.13.

Common quality assurance tasks should be treated long-term, and planning for them makes less sense during late phases of the project. There are mainly two reasons for this:

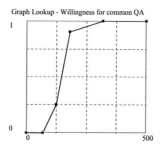

Figure 8.13.: Table function used in `Willingness for common QA`

1. The time required between planning and actual performance of common quality assurance tasks is long (compared to the case of regular communication tasks). The supplier should be given enough time to schedule the common activities. This time is on average 50 days in our model (compared to just 10 days in the case of regular communication tasks).

2. A significant portion of the positive effects of common quality assurance activities develop in the long-term. For example the benefits through the improved knowledge which the acquirer gets through these activities arise long-term, and also the benefits from an improved relationship to the supplier arise long-term.

The curve's shape results from the following assumptions regarding the acquirer's behavior: when less than $\frac{1}{10}$ of the project time is remaining then the acquirer is not willing to plan for any new common quality assurance activities. While the acquirer is fully willing to plan for quality assurance activities during the first third of the project, he slowly begins to hesitate during the second third of the project. We assume that the acquirer looses his willingness abruptly in the last third of the project.

Influences: `QA generation rate`

Value range: $[0, 1]$

- `QA execution rate`

Denotes the rate with which tasks for common quality assurance activities are executed by the staff of the acquirer project.

Formula: min(Tasks for common QA activities,

$$\frac{\text{Man Power for QA Activities}}{\text{actual Man-Days needed per QA task}} *$$

  Trust ratio)

The execution rate for common quality assurance tasks is dependent on the man power available which is represented through the variable Man Power for QA Activities. It is additionally dependent on how effective these tasks can be performed. This is expressed through the variable actual Man-Days needed per QA task which is – like in the case of regular communication tasks – dependent on the acquirer's technological knowledge; the better the know-how, the more effective the task performance for common quality assurance. But in contrast to the case of regular communication, this execution rate can be significantly hampered when the trust level is low. A distrustful supplier will surely not be cooperative in performing common reviews, common configuration management, or other common quality assurance activities. This is taken into account through the multiplication of the factor Trust ratio

Furthermore, the execution rate cannot be greater than the number of the current fixed tasks, and its amount is thus bounded by the level of the current common quality assurance tasks, i.e. through the level variable Tasks for common QA activities

Influences: Impl from tasks, Trust generation due to QA, Comprehension from Tasks, reported ratio

Value range: $[0, \sim 0.2]$

8.3.7. Man Power Allocation

In this part of the model, the man power of the project is adapted due to the demands arising from the planned tasks. For many variables in this part of the model, there exist two versions, one for each task type. We solely describe the variables belonging to the "common quality assurance"-task line; the respective variables for the "regular communication" case are defined analogously.

- Indicated WF level for QA activities

  Denotes the workforce level needed to work off all current quality assurance tasks in reasonable time.

Formula: $\dfrac{\texttt{Man-days for QA activities}}{\texttt{Max delay in QA activities}}$

The factor `Man-days for QA activities` shows the current amount of work for common quality assurance activities, i.e. it shows how many man-days are needed to work off all current planned tasks for common quality assurance (indicated through the level variable `tasks for common QA activities`).

The factor `Max delay in QA activities` indicates the time span during which a fixed quality assurance task should be executed. This should not be too long since planned activities get out of date after a certain amount of time, and it should not be too short since the supplier should be given enough time to schedule the common activities. The concrete number is highly dependent on the type of acquisition project and the concrete setting. We choose to set this factor to 50 days in our case. The respective value for the regular communication case, i.e. `Max delay in Regular Communication` should be set considerably lower: first, these are relative short interactions which have not to be scheduled by the supplier, and, second, they tend to get out of date faster than common quality assurance activities. We choose to set the respective factor for regular communication tasks to 10 days. But note again that the quantification of this factor very much depends on the concrete setting of the respective acquisition project.

The factor `Indicated WF level for QA activities` shows the workforce level with which the current fixed tasks could be worked off within `Max delay in QA activities` days. Thus, this is the workforce level the acquirer seeks to have for the execution of the common quality assurance tasks.

Influences: `Indicated WF level`,
`Fraction of MP for QA activities`

Value range: $[0, \sim2]$

- `Man power for QA activities`.

This variable denotes the man-power which will actually be spent on common quality assurance activities.

Formula: `Fraction of MP for QA Activities` $*$ `Total Workforce`
The `Fraction of MP for QA activities` indicates the man-power fraction (of the currently available man-power for the pro-

ject) which should be spent for common quality assurance activities and for regular communication, respectively. This fraction is determined on the basis of the indicated workforce level for common quality assurance activities and regular communication respectively.

The man power which will actually be spent for the common quality assurance activities is then the total workforce multiplied with `Fraction of MP for QA Activities`.

Influences: `QA execution rate`

Value range: $[0, \sim 2]$

- `Willingness to change WF level`

  Denotes the acquirer's willingness to change the workforce level at the given point in time.

  Formula: $\text{Lookup}(\frac{\texttt{Hiring Delay+Average Assimilation Delay}}{\texttt{Time remaining}})$
  with table function shown in figure 8.14.

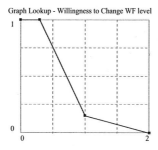

Figure 8.14.: Table function used in `Willingness to change WF level`

`Hiring Delay + Average Assimilation Delay` indicates the average time a new hiree requires to get fully productive. The table function thus plots the portion of the remaining time which an average new hiree needs to get fully productive against the willingness to change the workforce. An x-value of 0.25, for example, indicates that a new employee who would begin work at the given point in time would require on average a quarter of the remaining project time to get fully productive. An x-value of 1 and greater means accordingly that a newly hired employee would on average not succeed to get fully productive during the remaining project time.

We justify the shape of the table function through assuming the following hiring policy of the acquirer: when a newly hired employee needs less than a third of the remaining project time to get fully productive then the acquirer is fully willing to change the workforce. When this portion approaches the value 1, his willingness drops steadily to a low value. However, it is still not zero. Even if newly hired employees will not get fully productive, they still may support the existing workforce after they received some basic training. The willingness approaches zero when the time for getting fully productive gets twice as long as the remaining project time.

Influences: `WF needed`

Value range: $[0, 1]$

- `WF needed`

This factor indicates the workforce level needed as seen by the acquirer.

Formula: `Willingness to Change WF level` ∗
`Indicated WF level` + (1 −
`Willingness to Change WF level`) ∗ `Total Workforce`

The `Indicated WF level` specifies the workforce level which is actually needed to complete the tasks remaining (represented through the level variables `Tasks for common QA activities` and `Tasks for regular communication`) in reasonable time. In determining the value of the variable `WF needed`, the willingness to change the workforce level (i.e. `Willingness to Change WF level`) is taken into account; this willingness decreases when the project end gets close, or – more precisely – when the summation of the hiring and assimilation delay approaches the time remaining in the project.

Influences: `WF Level Sought`, `WF Gap` (indirectly)

Value range: $[0, \sim 6]$

- `Ceiling on New Hirees`

Denotes the maximum number of new hirees due to the number of experienced staff members.

Formula: `Experienced Workforce*`
　　　　`Most New Hirees Per Experienced Staff`

The work force level needed (`WF needed`) does not translate directly into the hiring goal. Management assesses the project's ability to absorb new people. We assume, like Abdel-Hamid and Madnick [1], a policy of project management, that restricts the rate of hiring new project members to the number that the experienced staff can handle, or, more precisely, what project management *thinks* that the experienced staff can handle. This limitation is formulated through the variable `Ceiling on New Hirees` which represents the number of the experienced staff multiplied with the variable `Most New Hirees Per Experienced Staff`. Like Abdel-Hamid and Madnick, we set the value of `Most New Hirees Per Experienced Staff` to 3.

Influences: `WF Level Sought`

Value range: $[0, \sim 10]$

8.3.8. Backbone

- `Acquirer's comprehension rate`

We assume here that the acquirer is aware of a great part of the requirements, but since he cannot completely think through the whole solution, he is not aware of them all. This factor determines the rate with which the acquirer discovers the requirements so far unconsidered.

Formula: `Acq's Technological Knowledge * littleness factor`

We assume here that the acquirer is aware of a great part of the requirements, but since he cannot completely think through the whole solution, he is not aware of them all. His technological knowledge (`Acq's Technological Knowledge`) helps to discover them. But it is a common observance that this is getting harder the fewer the undiscovered requirements get; this is accounted for through the `littleness factor` shown in figure 8.15. The number of requirements still not considered is plotted against it. The curve's shape is based on the following assumptions: when the number of undiscovered requirements is 100 (or greater) then the acquirer's comprehension rate will not be hampered; the `littleness-factor` has a value of 1. It starts to get more difficult for the acquirer when the number of undiscovered

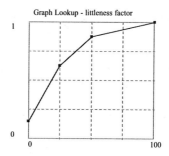

Figure 8.15.: The table function used in the `littleness factor` which is used in `Acquirer's comprehension rate`.

requirements gets lower than 100. The littleness-factor slowly begins to decrease, and, as the number of undiscovered requirements approaches zero, the decrease gets faster and faster.

Influences: `Reqs given to Supplier`

Value range: $[0, \sim 0.5]$

- `Supp's comprehension rate`

Determines the rate with which the supplier is able to comprehend the acquirer's needs and the requirements of the system to be acquired.

Formula: `Influence of pressure on comprehension` $* (1 -$ `actual unclarity`$) * ($`Basic comprehension rate` $+$ `Comprehension from Tasks`$)$

The comprehension rate is basically determined through the skills which the supplier brings into the project expressed through the variable `Basic comprehension rate`. But the comprehension rate can be considerably enhanced through direct interaction between acquirer and supplier; this prevents misunderstandings and may provide the acquirer's special domain knowledge to the supplier. The supplier's additional ability in comprehension stemming from the interaction of the acquirer and the supplier is represented through the variable `Comprehension from tasks`. So, we take the sum of the variables `Basic comprehension rate` and `Comprehension from tasks` as the basis for the formula calculating the comprehension rate.

We still have to consider two factors which may hamper (or support respectively) the supplier's comprehension:

- The application of pressure on the supplier influences the comprehension rate; slight pressure may support understanding, whereas too much pressure can hamper it. In order to account for this, we multiply the factor `Influence of pressure on comprehension` to the comprehension rate

- The supplier is missing a basis for having an overview when too many things are still unclear to him; a high level of unclarity hampers the comprehension rate. In order to account for this, we multiply the factor 1 − `actual unclarity` to the comprehension rate. (We assume here a strictly inversely proportional relationship in contrast to the case of the supplier's implementation rate, where the influence of the unclarity is stronger since the more dramatic implications of implementing the *wrong* things must be considered.)

Influences: `Reqs understood by supplier`

Value range: $[0, \sim 1]$

- `Supplier's implementation rate`

Determines the rate with which the supplier is able to implement the requirements of the system to be developed.

Formula: `Influence of pressure on implementation ∗`
`Unclarity Factor ∗ (Basic implementation rate +`
`Impl from Tasks)`

The reasoning here is for the most part analogous to the case the supplier's comprehension rate. Like the comprehension rate, the implementation rate is basically determined through the skills which the supplier brings into the project which is represented through the variable `Basic implementation rate`. The implementation rate can be enhanced through direct interaction between acquirer and supplier; this prevents misunderstandings and may provide the acquirer's special domain knowledge to the supplier (although this influence is lower than in the case of the supplier's comprehension rate). So, we take the sum of `Basic implementation rate` and `Implementation from Tasks` as the basis of the implementation rate.

There are still two factors which may hamper (or support respectively) the supplier's implementation rate:

– The application of pressure on the supplier influences the implementation rate – pretty much like its influence on the comprehension rate.

– When too many requirements are still unclear to the supplier, he runs the (great) risk of implementing the wrong things; this may imply in the worst case that the supplier uses his resources completely bootless, or it may at least entail lots of rework (which is, however, not explicitly modeled here). Compared to the case for the comprehension rate, the influence of the actual unclarity level is thus stronger here, and we use the table function `Unclarity Factor` to take this into account.

Influences: `Reqs implemented`

Value range: $[0, \sim 1]$

8.4. The Complete Model at a Glance

Figure 8.16 and figure 8.17 show the complete framework implementation at a glance (the model is too big to be shown in readable form in one single figure). Figure 8.16 shows the left part of the model representing the human resource management, and figure 8.17 shows the right part of the model which is the instance of the framework as presented in section 7.4.

Vensim slightly extends the system dynamics notation: names in brackets indicate variable links. Variable links allow models to be drawn simpler with a smaller amount of edge crossings. In figure 8.16, there are four variable links, namely "<actual Man-Days needed per comm. task>", "<actual Man-Days needed per QA task>", "<Tasks for regular communication>", and "<Tasks for common QA activities>". These variables are actually defined in the right part of the model shown in figure 8.17.

8.5. Model Outputs – "Answers" to the Problems

Section 7.1 presents the most common problems arising in the course of software acquisition projects. These problems play a central role in the design of the framework, and they are the matter on which the whole modeling effort

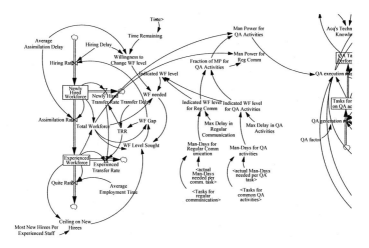

Figure 8.16.: An instance of the framework modeled with Vensim (left part).

is focused. This section tries to "answer" them through the examination of selected outputs of the system dynamics model presented before.

Most of these problems are about the impacts of a variation of a certain quantitative attribute: the impact of a *high* level of regular communication, the impact of a *high* level of common quality assurance activities, the impact of *high* pressure, the impact of a *badly* chosen supplier, and the impact of *low* technological knowledge of the acquirer. To get to the bottom of this kind of problems, we proceed as follows:

1. We perform at least two simulation runs[1] of the system dynamics model: one simulation run showing the course of the project when the attribute of interest is low, and, respectively, the other simulation run showing the course of the project when the respective attribute is high.

   This involves the variation of one or more parameters in the second simulation run depending on the number of parameters through which the aforementioned variation of the respective "quantitative attribute"

---

[1]In many cases, the model behaves monotonically (or at least monotonically) with respect to the variation of a specific attribute. In this case, two simulation runs are in fact sufficient. But there are cases where three runs seem to be more adequate like in section 8.5.3 when we analyze the consequences of severe pressure.

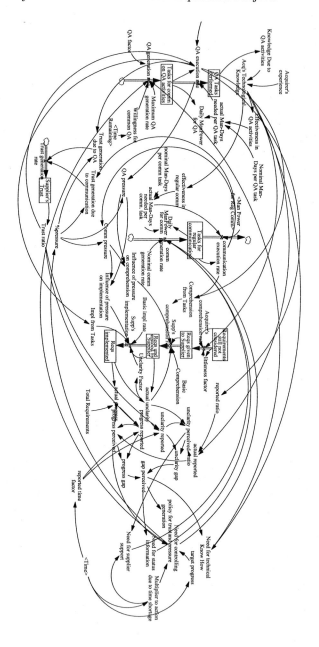

Figure 8.17.: An instance of the framework modeled with Vensim (right part).

can be performed.

2. We select the variables of the system dynamics model which are relevant with respect to the problem under consideration.

3. For each such variable, we compare its two graphs resulting from the two simulation runs; we derive an "answer" to the respective problem from these comparisons.

This approach cannot be applied, however, to the problem treated in subsection 8.5.5, namely the problem of preventing knowledge depletion; the problem there is not the consequence of the variation in a certain attribute but, vice versa, the question which variation is needed to get a certain course of a variable, namely a strongly rising "technological knowledge" variable.

8.5.1. Effectiveness of Regular Communication

In order to answer this question, we add – as shown in figure 8.18 – an additional constant factor to the "communication generation rate": the "regular communication factor". We simply multiply this factor to the original value

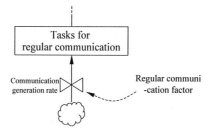

Figure 8.18.: An additional constant factor for the examination of the effectiveness of regular communication

of "Communication generation rate". In the simulation run which represents a high-communication policy, we set the value of "regular communication factor" to 1.0, and in the simulation run which represents a low-communication policy, we set its value to 0.5, i.e. in the high-communication case (which is the "normal" situation in the simulation model) there is twice as much communication than in the low-communication case.

Figure 8.19 shows differences in the graphs of selected variables between a low communication policy and a high communication policy. Figure 8.19(a)

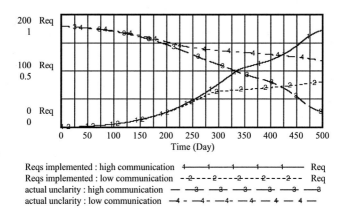

Reqs implemented : high communication ┼———┼———┼———┼———┼——— Req
Reqs implemented : low communication ─-2-─--2-─--2-─--2-─--2-─ Req
actual unclarity : high communication ── ─3─ ─3─ ─3─ ─3─ ─3─ ─3
actual unclarity : low communication ─4- ─4- —4- —4 — 4 — 4 —

(a) ... implementation and unclarity.

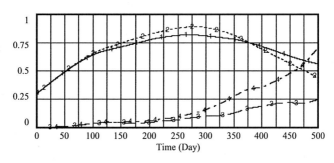

Supplier's Trust : high communication ─┼———┼———┼———┼———┼———┼─
Supplier's Trust : low communication ---2-─--2-─--2-─--2-─--2-─--2-
"%pressure" : high communication ─3———3———3———3—— 3 —— 3—— 3
"%pressure" : low communication ── -4— -4— -4— -4— -4— -4— -

(b) ... pressure and trust.

Figure 8.19.: Impact of regular communication on ...

shows the graphs of the implemented requirements and the unclarity, both indicators on the project's effectiveness. The "low-communication"-version of the "reqs implemented"-line shows a saturation towards the end at a significantly lower level than in the "high-communication"-version. The reason for this is that the supplier could not comprehend a sufficient amount of requirements in the course a the project with a low communication level. This can be seen through the graphs of the "actual unclarity" variable: too less communication implies that the unclarity stays high towards the end of the project – a direct consequence of too less communication between both parties.

Although secondary for the actual problem, the variables "Supplier's Trust" and "%pressure", whose graphs are shown in figure 8.19(b), are quite interesting with regards to further impacts of too less regular communication between the acquirer and the supplier. Too less communication makes the trust level more volatile; that means that the relationship with the supplier gets more sensitive to troubles, and the risk of overreactions in the case of disagreements increases.

We assume an acquirer who easily gets in panic when there is a serious threat of delay in the project's schedule – an assumption which is absolutely realistic with regards to our experience with real-world acquisition projects. It is therefore not surprising that – as figure 8.19(b) shows – the level of pressure strongly increases when communication gets low.

Furthermore, regarding the curves of all four variables, we notice the following: whereas there are nearly no deviations between the curves of the respective low-communication and high-communication case in the first half of the project, the consequences of bad communication seem to add up towards the end of the project, and the problems arising from bad communication seem to escalate; all curves strongly (a bit less in the case of the "Supp's Trust") diverge towards the project's end.

As an "answer" to the actual problem, we finally draw the conclusion – basing on the model outputs – that too less communication can be a significant cause for delay in the project's schedule.

8.5.2. Effectiveness of Common Quality Assurance

We model two forms of tasks concerning the interaction with the supplier: regular communication tasks whose effects on the acquisition project are analyzed in section 8.5.1 and common quality assurance tasks. Through regular communication, the acquirer's project and the supplier's project are coordinated and some open questions may be clarified. The execution of common quality assurance activities, on the other hand, is very different by its nature: it entails an intensive collaboration or even intervention in the supplier's project; the acquirer takes partial responsibility for the work done on the supplier side and gets more detailed hands-on information about the project's state. We therefore may well expect different results from a variation in the level of common quality assurance activities compared to the variation in the level of regular communication.

Similar to the last subsection, we add – as shown in figure 8.20 – an additional constant factor to the "QA generation rate", namely the "QA factor". We multiply this factor to the original value of "QA generation

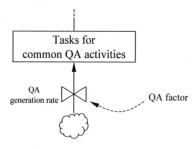

Figure 8.20.: An additional constant factor for the examination of the effectiveness of quality assurance activities.

rate". In the simulation run which represents a policy entailing a high level of common quality assurance activities, we set the value of "QA factor" to 1.0, and in the simulation run which represents a low-communication policy, we set its value to 0.3; that is, in the high-quality-assurance case (which is the "normal" situation in the simulation model) there are three times as much quality assurance activities than in the low-quality assurance case.

Figure 8.21 shows differences in the graphs of selected variables between a software acquisition project with a low level of common quality assurance activities and a project with a high level of common quality assurance activities. We expect benefits of a high level of common quality assurance activities; surprisingly, however, model outputs demonstrate the opposite: figure 8.21(a) shows that the project performance is clearly worse in the "high QA" case than in the "low QA" case. Furthermore, we can see from figure 8.21(b) that, in the "high QA" case, trust is nearly not present at the end of the project, whereas, in the "low QA" case, model outputs show a very solid trust on the supplier's side. Furthermore, the pressure is significantly

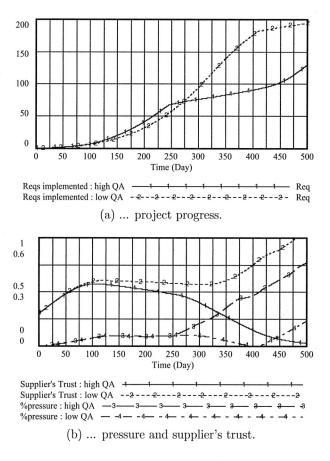

(a) ... project progress.

(b) ... pressure and supplier's trust.

Figure 8.21.: A weak acquirer: impact of common quality assurance on ...

higher in the "high QA" case.

These results seem to be counterintuitive; a closer look on the simulated acquirer and supplier reveals, however, that the results are reasonable: we modeled a quite inexperienced acquirer in combination with a quite competent supplier. The acquirer starts on a low level of technological knowledge, and he tends to overreact, when he is feared that the project gets late. Furthermore, a growing level of common quality assurance activities lets the acquirer see more details of the state of the supplier's project; an unskilled acquirer, however, runs the risk of misinterpreting the state of the project, and, in consequence, he runs the risk of taking the wrong decisions for "mitigation" of supposed problems which (amongst other things) entails a growing mistrust on the supplier's side – figure 8.21(b) confirms this. In this case, model outputs suggest the acquirer to keep out of the quality assurance activities of the supplier, provided the acquirer is much less skilled than the supplier since, in this case, common quality assurance will have a negative impact on the project's overall performance. If, however, one goal of the acquirer is to gain technological knowledge and knowledge in performing controlled acquisitions, then we have to rethink this advice since the execution of common quality assurance activities always – also in this case – entails a growth in knowledge.

We get a totally different view on the benefits of common quality assurance, when we model a competent supplier and a more stable acquisition project. We adapt the project scenario through changing the following parameters:

- *Pressure policy*: we model a more moderate form of pressure policy, which entails more moderate reactions to the threat of delays in project schedule.

- *Acquirer's technological knowledge*: we increase the initial level of the technological knowledge.

- *Acquirer's comprehension rate*: we increase the basic comprehension rate which results in an overall higher comprehension rate.

In the case of a competent supplier, who is capable of interpreting the signs he gets through common activities in a realistic and reasonable way, we get positive results from a growing level of common quality assurance not only on the acquirer's knowledge (cf. figure 8.22(b)) but also on the project's overall performance as indicated by the model outputs shown in figure 8.22(a): in the case of a high level of common quality assurance activities, nearly all requirements are implemented and the remaining unclarity is nearly zero after

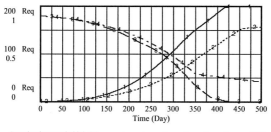

(a) ... implementation and unclarity.

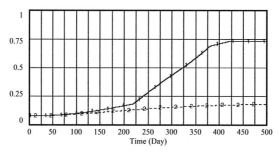

(b) ... the acquirer's technological knowledge.

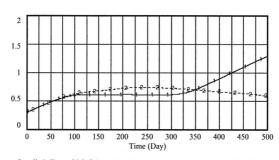

(c) ... the supplier's trust level.

Figure 8.22.: An experienced acquirer: impact of common quality assurance on ...

400 days, i.e.the project is nearly in time[2]. Basing on the the more detailed observations from the high level of common activities, an experienced supplier draws useful conclusions about the project's state, and, consequently, he takes reasonable decisions. This, in turn, creates trust on the supplier's side – the model outputs shown in figure 8.22(c) demonstrate this.

We finally conclude that a high level of common quality assurance activities always has positive effects on the acquirer's technological know-how. Provided that the acquirer is sufficiently experienced in performing software acquisition projects, we also can expect positive effects on the projects overall performance when a high level of common quality assurance activities is ensured. If, however, the acquirer is not skilled in acquisition projects and (respectively or) in the respective technical issues, then model outputs suggest the acquirer to keep out of the supplier's quality assurance – provided, at least, that the goal is solely a performant project and not the gain of knowledge on the acquirer's side.

8.5.3. Consequences of Severe Pressure

We multiplied a "pressure factor" to the variable "%pressure" (cf. section 8.3.5 for its definition – this variable results from needs arising from the acquirer's perception of the backbone). The "low pressure"-policy results from setting the "pressure-factor" to 0.3, the "high pressure"-policy results from setting it to 1, and the "severe pressure'-policy results from setting it to 3, i.e. "high pressure" means approximately three times as much pressure as "low pressure", and "severe pressure" means three times as much pressure as "high pressure". Figure 8.23 shows the output graphs of three model variables, the requirements implemented, the workforce level, and the supplier's trust level; for each variable, three graphs are shown, one for each of the above mentioned pressure policies.

Figure 8.23(a) shows that the high pressure policy is most ineffective in terms of the project's progress; approximately a third of the requirements has not been implemented after 500 days. The low, i.e. moderate, pressure policy shows the best results; after 450 days, all requirements are implemented and the project is nearly in time. Surprisingly, also the severe pressure policy seems to be quite effective, at least with respect to the implemented requirements. However, it is not effective in terms of costs: the work force level which is needed in a severe pressure project is much higher – specially in the

---

[2]As mentioned earlier, we always model late acquisition projects which are, with regards to our experience, the "normal" case; so, whereas the time-scale covers 500 days, the expected closure of the project is after 400 days.

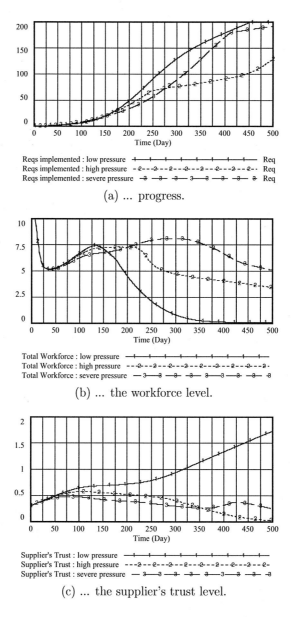

(a) ... progress.

(b) ... the workforce level.

(c) ... the supplier's trust level.

Figure 8.23.: Impact of severe pressure on ...

last two thirds of the projects – than in projects with more moderate pressure application. Figure 8.23(b) indicates that the more pressure is applied, the more man power is needed (i.e. the more costly the project gets) on the acquirer side for interaction with the supplier. The great divergence in the curves representing the work force level for different pressure policies are effects of a positive feedback loop: too much pressure lowers the supplier's capabilities which, in turn, brings the acquirer to apply even higher pressure which results in more monitoring and controlling effort and, in consequence, a higher work force level. After the first third of the project time has passed, the reinforcing loop takes effect and lets the lines diverge.

Severe pressure has negative impacts not only on the project's costs but also on the supplier's trust towards the acquirer and the supplier's general mindset towards the project. Figure 8.23(c) shows that the acquirer has to face a dramatic drop in his partner's trust when he increases pressure.

We conclude that model outputs advise to apply solely moderate pressure[3] on the supplier. Whereas the acquisition project's progress may not be hampered by severe pressure, and the project costs the supplier's trust always suffer from too much pressure application.

8.5.4. Consequences of Unheeding Supplier Selection

The framework, and consequently this system dynamics model, does not include the supplier selection process due to various reasons (cf. section 7.4.1). Nevertheless, we can model the consequences of an unheeding supplier selection process: the course of an acquisition project with a less competent supplier compared to the course of an acquisition project with a competent supplier.

The system dynamics model representing a less competent supplier is modified in two parameters:

- Supplier's comprehension rate: this variable is lowered 30%.

- Supplier's implementation rate: this variable is lowered 20%.

We suppose here, that the supplier's weaknesses have a slightly greater effect on the requirements' comprehension rate than on the implementation rate

---

[3]It may seem problematic to characterize pressure as "moderate", since pressure can hardly be quantified. It helps to interpret the advices basing on the model outputs vice versa: when the acquirer faces a low trust level, too high project costs, and the risk of delays, then reducing pressure can help to mitigate these problems.

since we suppose that "competency" is more a question of familiarity in the respective domain than a question of implementation capabilities.

Model outputs indicating the impact of an unheeding supplier selection process, that is the impact of an incompetent supplier, are shown in figure 8.24. Expectedly, implications are dramatic despite the comparatively slight changes made in the model representing the incompetent supplier: figure 8.24(a) shows that an unheeding supplier selection implies a dramatic drop in the acquisition's effectiveness. The outputs shown in figure 8.24(b) are also not surprising: the trust level of the incompetent supplier is much lower – specially at the end of the project – than the trust level of the competent supplier. This is because the insufficient competencies of the supplier cause the acquirer to increase pressure which results – at least in this case – in a low trust level.

8.5.5. Knowledge Depletion

In this subsection, we deal with the question, how knowledge depletion could be prevented. This question is more difficult to answer than the questions treated in the preceding subsections where we could simply add a multiplier to the variable under consideration. In this case, we have to find out the factors which actually influence knowledge growth and knowledge depletion respectively

Prevention of Knowledge Depletion

The question, how knowledge depletion could be prevented, or, in other words, how the acquirer's level of technological knowledge could be improved, has partly been answered in section 8.5.2: figure 8.22 shows that a growing level of common quality assurance activities entails a noticeable growth in the acquirer's knowledge.

Since we decided, based on the deductive and inductive reasoning of section 7.4, to model common quality assurance as the only factor influencing the growth of the acquirer's technological knowledge, increasing the level of common quality assurance activities is the only (direct) way to prevent knowledge depletion in his system dynamics model. Common quality assurance is the thus key for preventing knowledge depletion.

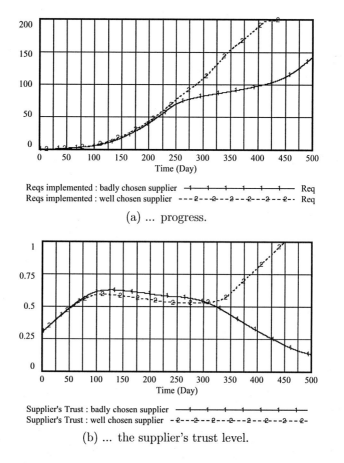

(a) ... progress.

(b) ... the supplier's trust level.

Figure 8.24.: Impact of an unheeding supplier selection process on ...

Consequences of Knowledge Depletion

In order to model the consequences of knowledge depletion, we modify the influence of the execution of common quality assurance. This influence is expressed via a table function (cf. section 8.3.3). Figure 8.25(a) shows the table function for the "high knowledge" case and figure 8.25(b) shows the table function for the "low knowledge" case.

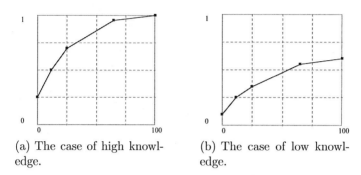

(a) The case of high knowledge.

(b) The case of low knowledge.

Figure 8.25.: Table functions modeling the impact of the execution of common quality assurance activities on technological knowledge.

The influence of knowledge on the project's effectiveness is clearly shown in figure 8.26(a): if the acquirer makes arrangements against knowledge depletions then the project is nearly in time. On the other hand, if the acquirer has less know-how, then not all requirements could be implemented after 500 work days. It is also not surprising that the supplier's trust level (at least at the end of the project) is much lower when the supplier has to deal with an technically unskilled acquirer.

8.6. Model Validity

The implications of questions like "Is the model valid?" or "Has the model been validated?" is that validation is a one time action that takes place after a model is built and before it is used. However, model validation is always a process and its validity cannot be instantly proved in a mathematical sense. Nevertheless, we can provide first indications on the model's validity based on the material presented in this chapter.

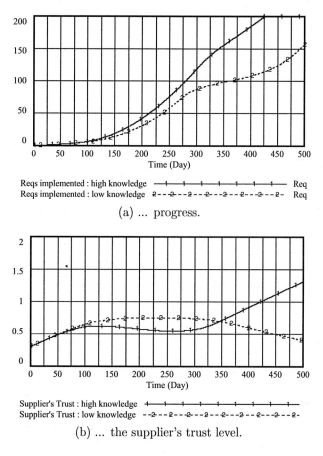

(a) ... progress.

(b) ... the supplier's trust level.

Figure 8.26.: Impact of knowledge depletion on ...

We adhere to Richardson and Pugh [66] who suggest that the validity of a (system dynamics) model should be made up of two questions:

1. Is the model *suitable* for its purposes and the problem it addresses: One cannot judge the validity of a model without having clearly in mind the goals of a modeling project. Section 8.6.1 analyses to what extent the modeling goals are achieved through the system dynamics model presented in this chapter.

2. Is the model consistent with the respective part of reality? According to Richardson and Pugh, the validity of a system dynamics model is closely related with the model's capability to reproduce the reference behavior modes. Section 8.6.2 compares the reference behavior modes with respective model outputs.

8.6.1. Modeling Purposes and Their Achievements

One cannot judge the validity of a model without having clearly in mind the goals of a modeling project. As a metaphor, Richardson and Pugh [66] use Lewis Caroll's observation that a clock that never runs is more accurate than a clock that loses a minute a day: the stopped clock shows the right time twice a day, the late clock, however, shows the right time only about once every two years. But which clock constitutes a more valid model of time? The answer depends on its actual purpose. And its purpose is not to be exactly right, but to help its owner get to appointments on time; more generally speaking, its purpose is not point prediction but behavior prediction.

Similarly, the purpose of the system dynamics model and the modeling project described here is not point prediction. As already mentioned in section 6.4, we need no exact quantitative prognoses for our objectives. The goal is rather behavior predication. Our aim of this modeling project is actually twofold: first, we want to raise consciousness of critical behavior of software acquisition projects and, second, we want to better understand the overall behavior of software acquisition projects. The validity of the system dynamics model presented in this chapter has to be measured against the achievement of these two aims.

Consciousness Raising

We need a tool to raise consciousness. This tool should corroborate our advices; it has to impart our experiences about what really matters in software acquisitions, what the main success factors are, and where common causes for failure can be found. And indeed, our experiences about problematic behavior in software acquisition projects, which are also confirmed in literature [47, 67], are supported by model outputs:

- Software acquisition projects can be – often against intuition of the involved parties – difficult and frequently overrun time and budget, specially when the acquirer has little experience and underestimates risks. Model outputs corroborate this: figure 8.21 and figure 8.26 show that weaknesses on the acquirer's side have dramatic (and even unexpected) consequences on project performance.

- The acquirer should strive for regular communication and a fine granular coordination with the supplier. Good communication between both parties fosters a better relationship and a more open atmosphere; problems are identified earlier and possible cost and time overruns may be prevented. Model outputs corroborate this: figure 8.22 and figure 8.19 show the severe consequences of too less cooperation.

- Is is worth while to select the supplier carefully, even if this might take lots of time. The supplier selection process is a critical step in software acquisition projects. Model outputs corroborate this: figure 8.24 shows that a badly chosen supplier could do a lot of harm to project performance.

- Knowledge depletion is a major risk for the acquirer and it should be prevented (for example through common quality assurance activities with the supplier) even if it costs resources. A good technological knowledge base of the acquirer positively impacts the overall project performance. Model outputs corroborate this as shown in figure 8.26.

Through this system dynamics model, we have a powerful tool to argue for our advices. What regards consciousness raising, the model is thus valid.

Understanding

The issues of "Consciousness Raising" and "Understanding" overlap. The model's capability to raise consciousness for important aspects of acquisition projects also means that it is capable of helping the project's staff in understanding software acquisition. However, the issue of "Understanding" here, includes a more extensive point of view: we ask, if the model can even deliver surprising results to the modelers themselves who are – as we assume here –

more aware and knowledgeable of possible problems in software acquisition than the project's staff and the project management.

In fact, it can deliver surprising results: figure 8.21 shows model outputs which are, at first sight, neither reasonable nor obvious. They are only with hindsight explicable after thoroughly thinking the things through. This leads the modeler and the model user to rethink the hypotheses, which have been incorporated into the model, and to rethink the conclusions which so far were drawn based in common sense and which now probably have to be adapted to more adequate conclusions with regards to the respective hypotheses.

The outputs shown in figure 8.21 are, of course, no proof, but they are a strong hint that the model is coherent enough to be capable of helping modelers and model users to gain a better understanding of acquisition projects. The model seems to achieve the issue of "Understanding".

8.6.2. Reference Behavior Modes Revisited

The reference behavior modes are part of the specification of a system dynamics model; they describe the problem behavior of the part of reality to be modeled in terms of graphs of variables over time. Figure 7.1(a) and figure 7.1(b) on page 111 show the reference behavior modes for "problematic" behavior in software acquisition projects. Figure 7.1(a) shows an unfavorable course of a late software acquisition project in terms of the actual, the reported, and the perceived progress, and figure 7.1(b) shows an more favorable course of a late acquisition projects in terms of the same variables.

In this section, we analyze the question if the system dynamics model presented in this chapter is capable of reproducing these reference behavior modes, i.e. we search for hints indicating that the model is consistent with the respective part of reality. For this, we have to represent a "favorable" project and an "unfavorable" project; in our model, they differ in the following respects:

1. The acquirer is experienced, i.e. he has a higher initial technological and project knowledge.

2. He gains knowledge faster through a better exchange with the supplier, i.e. the level of common activities is higher.

3. The relationship to the supplier is better, i.e. the supplier's trust level is higher and less volatile.

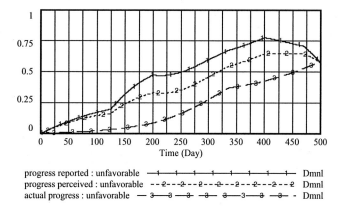

progress reported : unfavorable —1—1—1—1—1—1—1—1— Dmnl
progress perceived : unfavorable --2---2--2--2---2--2--2---2--2 Dmnl
actual progress : unfavorable — 3—3—3—3—3—3—3—3— - Dmnl

(a) The course of an unfavorable acquisition project in terms of reported, perceived, and actual progress.

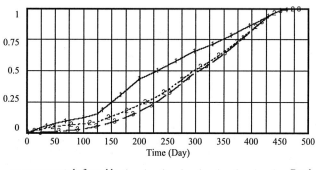

progress reported : favorable 1—1—1—1—1—1—1—1—1— Dmnl
progress perceived : favorable 2--2--2---2--2--2---2--2--2---2 Dmnl
actual progress : favorable 3— 3— 3— 3—3 —3— 3— 3—3 — Dmnl

(b) The course of a favorable acquisition project in terms of reported, perceived, and actual progress.

Figure 8.27.: Reference behavior modes revisited.

Figure 8.27 shows the model outputs which we compare to the reference behavior modes: figure 8.27(a) corresponds to the behavior mode shown in figure 7.1(a), and figure 8.27(b) corresponds to the behavior mode shown in figure 7.1(b).

The first thing attracting attention is that the model reproduces the reference behavior mode of the favorable course of an acquisition project very closely; this is shown in figure 8.27(b). The progress perceived by the acquirer soon converges with the actual progress, and the acquirer is capable of reacting to problems in time. This makes the difference between the reported progress and the actual progress less than in the case of the "unfavorable" project.

The output which the model produces for the unfavorable course of an acquisition project is also similar to the corresponding reference behavior mode; there is a huge gap in the reported/perceived progress and, for a quite long time, the progress perceived by the acquirer is too much oriented towards the progress reported by the supplier; the acquirer's actions to mitigate problems thus come too late. There is a minor difference to the reference behavior mode shown in figure 7.1(a), however: we model a project with a rigid time limit whereas the project shown in the reference behavior mode runs until all (or nearly all) requirements have been implemented. Neglecting this rather technical difference, we can safely say that the system dynamics model also reproduces the second reference behavior mode.

Eventually, we conclude that model outputs provide strong hints that the model is consistent with the respective part of reality due to its capability to reproduce both reference behavior modes.

8.7. Concluding Remarks

It is difficult – in fact, some think it is impossible – to base the development of a concrete system dynamics model of a *human* system on a sound scientific fundament. Many unproven hypotheses flow into the quantitative and also into the structural design. And in the end, the simulation outputs simply reflect the respective hypotheses; so, from a scientific point of view, we can neither fully trust system dynamics models of human systems, nor their respective outputs.

In contrast to other system dynamics modeling projects described in literature (e.g. [3, 15, 16, 53, 51, 60, 71, 72, 83]), we mitigate these shortfalls through the following proceeding:

1. Before modeling a concrete project, we first try to capture common structures of all system dynamics models of software acquisition projects; this results in the framework described in chapter 7. We base the system dynamics model described in this chapter on this framework. Thereby, we have a more robust fundament of the model's structural design. The model's actual quantification, however, remains hypothetical (which, in fact, is inherent in models of human systems).

2. We stick to the modeling process suggested in the renowned literature [66], which includes a (kind of) requirements phase: we specify the models' purpose, we specify the models' scope through stating the problems of interest, and we specify the models' behavior through stating reference behavior modes (cf. section 7.1).

3. The fact that the framework's design (and, thus, also the model's design) is based on clearly stated requirements enables us to perform a verification – which is, admittedly, not purely formal – of the model's validity against these requirements.

This is probably neither the only valid way to model software acquisition projects nor can the validity of the presented model be formally proven in a mathematical sense. But this chapter provides strong hints (which is, in fact, all we can expect) that the model is useful, valid, and consistent with the respective part of reality.

Part IV.

Combinations

Chapter 9

Combining Process-Oriented Interactive Simulation with System Dynamics

In this chapter, we describe an approach to combine the process-oriented interactive simulation technique described in part II and System Dynamics, particularly the system dynamics model treated in part III. At first glance, these two simulation techniques seem to be incompatible: the process-oriented interactive simulation technique has a defined process as its basis consisting of a set of ordered process steps which should be performed in order to acquire a software product. This is a discontinuous view on software acquisition. On the other hand, System Dynamics employs a continuous view on a system: behavior is specified through continuous laws which are valid during the whole simulated time span; a fixed set of dynamic rules is producing the system's behavior. In System Dynamics, there is therefore no such thing like an underlying process. This chapter tries to integrate these incompatible paradigms.

We do *not* seek to present a readily implementable simulation system in full detail here. There are several reasons for this:

- Any treatment beyond this scope would describe straight and technical implementational details. Too many uninteresting – uninteresting at least from a scientific point of view – technical details would be required to present.

- The implementation techniques, namely the process-oriented interactive simulation and system dynamics modeling, have already been presented in previous chapters. An in-depth treatment of the implementation would thus entail redundancy.

We merely present a "cookbook" containing instructions how to use the facts coded in a system dynamics model in building an interactive simulation. In section 9.2, we present an approach to combine the two paradigms, and, in section 9.3, we present a concrete high-level example for a combination of a part of the system dynamics model (developed in part III) with an example description of the software acquisition process in HFSP notation which is presented in section 9.1.

9.1. Example Process

In this section, we present an example process in extended HFSP notation which is introduced in section 5.4.1; we already presented a simpler description of the software acquisition process in figure 5.3 on page 73. But here, we need are more detailed process description in order to demonstrate in section 9.3 how to combine System Dynamics and the interactive simulation on the basis of a concrete example.

As already mentioned in section 5.4.1, process steps marked with a $\mathcal{P}$ are *passive*, i.e. the player (taking the role of the leader of the acquisition project) has to activate them, and process steps marked with an $\mathcal{A}$ are *active*, i.e. their initiation does not come from the player, but they rather activate themselves. In addition to the HFSP extensions described in section 5.4.1, we invent a third tag, namely $\mathcal{A}^{st}$. Process steps marked with $\mathcal{A}^{st}$ – *st* stands for "staff" – are executed partially or completely by the staff, not by the project manager (i.e. the player) himself; the player executes them just indirectly through instructing his staff to perform the respective process steps.

Types:

> concrete-supplier, contract, request-for-proposal,
> sw-product, requirements, project-plan, project-plan-supplier,
> CM-infrastructure, staff

Activities:

procure-software (| sw-product) $\Rightarrow$
$\mathcal{P}$ **establish-project-plan** (| project-plan)
$\mathcal{P}$ **assemble-staff** (| staff)
$\mathcal{P}$ **elicit-requirements** (staff | requirements)
     tendering (staff | concrete-supplier)
$\mathcal{P}$ **prepare-contract** (concrete-supplier |

concrete-supplier, contract, sw-product)
monitor-supplier (concrete-supplier, contract,
                sw-product, requirements, project-plan, staff |
            concrete-supplier, contract,
            sw-product, requirements, project-plan)
$\mathcal{A}$ **acquisition-acceptance** (concrete-supplier, contract,
                    sw-product, requirements, staff |
                    sw-product)
manage-project (project-plan, staff | project-plan, staff)

procure-software (| sw-product) $\Rightarrow$
$\mathcal{P}$ **buy-Cots-product** (| sw-product)

monitor-supplier (concrete-supplier, contract,
                sw-product, requirements, project-plan, staff |
             concrete-supplier, contract,
             sw-product, requirements, project-plan) $\Rightarrow$
$\mathcal{A}$ **contract-change-mgmt** (concrete-supplier, contract, staff |
                    concrete-supplier, contract)
common-QA-activities (concrete-supplier, sw-product, requirements, staff |
                    concrete-supplier, sw-product, requirements)
regular-communication (concrete-supplier, project-plan, staff |
                    concrete-supplier, project-plan)

tendering (staff | concrete-supplier) $\Rightarrow$
$\mathcal{P}$ **prepare-rfp** (staff | request-for-proposal)
$\mathcal{P}$ **issue-rfp** (request-for-proposal staff | request-for-proposal)
$\mathcal{A}$ **select-supplier** (request-for-proposal staff | concrete-supplier)

manage-project (project-plan, staff | project-plan, staff) $\Rightarrow$
$\mathcal{P}$ **audit-project-mgmt** (project-plan | project-plan)
$\mathcal{P}$ **organize-training** (project-plan, staff | project-plan, staff)
$\mathcal{P}$ **project-meeting** (project-plan, staff | project-plan, staff)
$\mathcal{P}$ **project-planning** (project-plan | project-plan)
$\mathcal{P}$ **communicate-with-staff** (staff | staff)
$\mathcal{P}$ **monitor-and-control-staff** (staff project-plan | staff)
$\mathcal{A}^{st}$ **staff-communicates** (staff | staff)
$\mathcal{P}$ **risk-mgmt** (project-plan, staff | project-plan, staff)

common-QA-activities (concrete-supplier, sw-product, requirements, staff |
concrete-supplier, sw-product, requirements) ⇒
$\mathcal{A}^{st}$ **start-joint-config-mgmt** (concrete-supplier, staff | CM-infrastructure)
$\mathcal{A}^{st}$ **perform-joint-config-mgmt** (concrete-supplier, sw-product,
CM-infrastructure, staff |
concrete-supplier, sw-product)
$\mathcal{A}^{st}$ **review-suppliers-pm** (concrete-supplier, project-plan-supplier, staff |
concrete-supplier, project-plan-supplier)
$\mathcal{A}^{st}$ **joint-SW-review** (concrete-supplier, sw-product, staff |
concrete-supplier, sw-product)
$\mathcal{P}$ **joint-risk-mgmt** (concrete-supplier staff | concrete-supplier)

regular-communication (concrete-supplier, project-plan, staff |
concrete-supplier, project-plan) ⇒
$\mathcal{P}$ **communicate-requirements** (concrete-supplier, requirements, staff |
concrete-supplier, requirements)
$\mathcal{P}$ **coordinate-joint-activities** (project-plan,
project-plan-supplier, concrete-supplier |
project-plan, project-plan-supplier)
$\mathcal{P}$ **foster-good-relationship** (concrete-supplier | concrete-supplier)

Figure 9.1.: The process which forms the basis of the interactive simulation
using the system dynamics framework. In extended HFSP notation.

The programmer of an interactive simulation surely has to be concerned
about the way the tags $\mathcal{P}$, $\mathcal{A}$, and $\mathcal{A}^{st}$ are realized in the implementation.
If active process steps are possibly realized via a an internal timer, a ran-
domly driven activation, or what type of announcement is chosen when an
active process step is activated is subject to the taste of the designer of the
simulation game. In this dissertation, we abstract the concrete treatment
of the tags of the process steps and rather concentrate on the integration of
System Dynamics in the interactive simulation methodology.

9.2. An Approach for Combining Processes and System Dynamics

A system dynamics simulation run is monolithic and predetermined. An
interactive simulation run, on the other hand, must *neither* be monolithic
nor predetermined; it must be discontinuous, interrupted by the player's

actions, and – characteristic to every game – the simulation's course must be largely determined by the player's actions.

Thus, the first step in combining System Dynamics with process-oriented interactive simulation is to open system dynamics models for interruptions. System dynamics models have to be somehow made discontinuous – at least at selected points. In other words, they have to be "opened" for the decisions of the player[1]. In the following, we call the points in system dynamics models which are opened for the player's decisions "discontinuations" or "*unstitches*", and we call the process of making a system dynamics model discontinuous "discontinuing" or "*unstitching*".

9.2.1. Unstitching System Dynamics Models

How can system dynamics models be made discontinuous? Which structures in system dynamics models can be associated with unstitches? We get an answer to these questions when we consider that we simply need to model a new form of influence which cannot be expressed in System Dynamics, namely influences emerging from actions of a player. It is reasonable to enhance the influences representable in System Dynamics with this new form of influence. In System Dynamics, influences are expressed as information flows and material flows, and, therefore, we attach unstitches to information flows and material flows. Figure 9.2 shows the additional syntax we are using in the rest of this chapter for adding unstitches to system dynamics models.

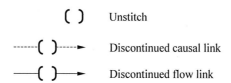

Figure 9.2.: Syntax for adding discontinuations to system dynamics models

So far, an unstitch expresses that there is some kind of additional influence taking effect in an information flow or a material flow respectively. However, we do not only need a way to express *that* there is some kind of influence, we also need a way to express *what* kind of influence that is. Now, the crucial

---

[1]Although these ideas seem to be obvious, the author does not know of any approaches for combining interactive simulation with System Dynamics described in literature.

step in combining the process-oriented interactive simulation methodology and System Dynamics is to associate an unstitch with an adequate process step function of the interactive simulation. The additional syntax needed to express these associations is shown in figure 9.3.

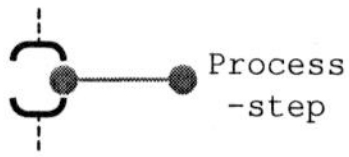

Process   Discontinuation bridged by
-step   process step function `Process-step`

Figure 9.3.: Syntax for associating process step functions to discontinuations

9.2.2. Implementing Unstitches

It remains to clarify what an unstitch associated with a process step function actually means, and how it affects a simulation run. This meaning is most effectively specified through describing possible realizations of the syntax described in figure 9.2 and figure 9.3. There are basically two possibilities for realization:

1. The system dynamics model dominates: this results in a real-time simulation. The simulated time continuously passes – slow enough that the player is able to interact –, and all model variables are continuously changing due to the information and material flow specified in the system dynamics model. Each time the player executes a process step function, the influences in the system dynamics model are updated due to the specified unstitches.

2. The process model dominates: this results in a non-real-time simulation. The simulated time does not pass continuously; it passes abruptly each time the player executes a process step. With each execution of a process step, the underlying system dynamics model runs for a certain amount of time – whereas the amount of time could be dependent on the process step which is currently executed. In addition to all dynamic rules specified in the underlying system dynamics model, the influences of the executed process step take effect in this partial run. They actually take effect at all points in the system dynamics model which are marked with an unstitch associated with the currently executed process step function.

The process-oriented interactive simulation method described in part II is generic with respect to the underlying techniques to describe the low-level project dynamics. So, both aforementioned realizations may use the process-oriented interactive simulation technique with its process interpreter (see section 5.4.3) as the tool to offer the player the process steps for execution.

9.2.3. Criteria for Unstitching Flows

An important issue remains to be clarified: obviously, not all information flows and material flows in system dynamics models are suitable for unstitching.

The influences expressed in system dynamics models of human systems can basically be classified in two groups: first, influences expressing direct causality or inevitability; unstitching information or material flows which express this kind of information makes no sense. The second group comprises influences which incorporate human behavior; this kind of influence is effective under the assumption that a certain way of behavior holds for a group of persons involved in the system. Solely this kind of influence is suitable for unstitching.

For example, unstitching the information flow from the level variable "Requirements implemented" to the auxiliary "actual progress" (this flow is depicted in figure 7.7 on page 120) makes no sense, since this influence is purely calculational: no endeavor neither by the supplier nor by the acquirer is needed to make this information flow work; this causality rather expresses inevitability.

An example of an influence belonging to the second group is the information flow from "Need for controlling & pressure" to "QA generation rate" (this flow is depicted in figure 7.6 on page 118 and in figure 9.4 on page 202). It vitally depends on the abilities of the project manager to lead and to instruct the project staff to implement that need.

9.3. Example

It is reasonable to build the combinations and unstitch the feedback structures on the level of the system dynamics framework, and not on the level of a concrete implementation: as possible it is to make generalizations with regard to structure of system dynamics models of acquisition projects as possible it is to make generalizations with regard to the locations where it might be reasonable to unstitch feedback structures. Even though the unstitches are dependent on the process which one seeks to fuse with the system dynamics model, for one concrete process, however, it makes sense to consider the unstitches on the framework level.

9.3.1. Unstitching the Tasks Diagram

As an example for unstitching system diagrams, we present one possible way to unstitch the task diagram treated in section 7.4.4 on page 117. The process steps associated with the unstitches base on the example software acquisition process presented in section 9.1. Figure 9.4 shows the unstitched tasks diagram.

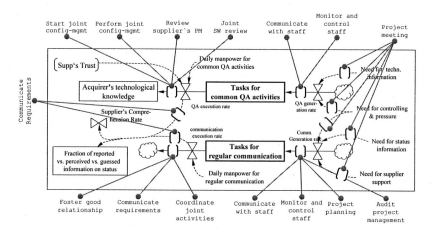

Figure 9.4.: The unstitched tasks component

We begin with the right part of figure 9.4 in explaining the unstitches. As already explained on page 118, the needs – need for technical know-how, need for controlling and pressure, need for status information, and need for supplier support – determine the values of the task generation rates, or, in a terminology more suitable to project management, they determine how many tasks are scheduled. In the system dynamics model, this influence is depicted through a simple causal link. All the management tasks that have to be ably performed in order to make this link "work" are hidden; system dynamics abstracts it. In reality, having the respective needs in mind, the project manager has to communicate them to his staff and instruct the staff to take appropriate action, namely scheduling tasks in this case – we assume here that the staff is responsible for planning the common quality assurance activities. It is, thus, reasonable to unstitch the respective causal links. We associate the unstitches to the process step "Project meeting"; project meetings, we assume, are the medium to inform and brief the staff. The unstitch introduces a further dependency: the way the needs are passed on to the task generation rates depends on the abilities of the project manager to lead the project meetings and instruct the staff members.

The task generation rates open the material flow – in this case, the "material" consists of the tasks – into the task levels. Similar to the case of the information links from the needs to the task generation rate, the material flow hides many details: in real project life, this flow actually is performed through planning activities by both the project's staff and – in the case of the regular communication tasks – also by the project manager. We can express this fact through unstitching the material flow. What process steps should be associated with these unstitches? As the project manager, the player has to insure himself, if the staff members really do what they were told to do, i.e. if they really plan, if they plan the right tasks, and if they plan the tasks thoroughly; as regards this insurance, the process steps "Communicate with staff" and "Monitor and control staff" are crucial, and they are therefore associated with these unstitches.

Clearly, many activities are associated with the execution of tasks. In System Dynamics, however, important for project simulation is solely the fact that (and when) the tasks are executed; the question how in detail the tasks are performed is ignored in the system dynamics model. The player of the simulation has to be able to influence the quality of the task execution, and we unstitch the outflow of the task levels. The unstitch of the common quality assurance tasks outflow is obviously associated with process steps representing common quality assurance activities, namely "Start joint config-mgmt", "Perform joint config-mgmt", "Review supplier's PM", and "Joint SW review". The unstitch of the regular communication outflow the process steps "Foster good relationship", "Communicate requirements", and "Coordinate joint activities".

The exact way the requirements are communicated to the supplier surely influences the supplier's comprehension rate; thus, we unstitch the information links from the task execution rates to the supplier's comprehension rate and associate the unstitch with the process step "Communicate requirements".

9.4. Concluding remarks

One usually tries to approach the task of designing a simulation game in a bottom-up manner; that is, small things are modeled and the focus is on emergent behavior. The SESAM simulation system is an example for such an approach.

In combining System Dynamics with the process-oriented interactive simulation technique, however, the focus shifts towards a top-down view of the simulated domain. The basis is the high-level process which guides the player in interacting with the simulation system; the basis is not the modeling of the small entities forming the simulated domain.

Part V.

Epilogue

Chapter 10

Contributions

There are different perspectives to view the contributions of this dissertation. First, there are the contributions for the respective scientific communities, namely the software process modeling community, the system dynamics simulation community, and the interactive software process modeling community. These specific contributions are presented in section 10.1.

Viewing this dissertation as a whole, we can, first, regard the contribution as the invention and application of techniques for imparting process knowledge; section 10.2 goes into details. Second, we can regard the contribution as the construction of a basis for developing a simulation game of the software acquisition process. Section 10.3 presents this view.

10.1. Contributions for the Scientific Communities

This dissertation seeks to be self-contained and things are therefore comprehensively introduced. So, the contributions for the respective scientific communities are scattered over the dissertation. The following listing presents the most important contributions; references showing where these contributions are presented and a short description are additionally provided with each contribution.

- *Designing GARP*

    Brief Description: An acquisition model is designed which fulfills the requirements "comprehensiveness", "(temporal) ordered process steps", and "sufficient detailing". Although it bases on many existing process models, its architecture is novel and it is – to the authors knowledge – the first effort in designing a model which fulfills these three requirements. This contribution has been presented at the 7th European Conference on Software Quality and is published in the Lecture Notes in Computer Science series [36].

Location: Section 3.2 (but actually, the whole chapter 3 is an extended version of the respective publication [36]).

- *Interactive Simulation*

  Brief Description: A process-oriented and functional approach to interactive simulation is presented. There have been previous attempts to interactively simulate software processes [50, 88] but this is a novel approach. It uses ideas from the functional programming paradigm and even from compiler construction and raises the process step to the status of a "first-class citizen". This process-oriented approach to interactive simulation allows to map process models like GARP straightforwardly to an interactive simulation. This contribution has been presented at the First Eurasian Conference on Information and Communication Technology and is published in the Lecture Notes in Computer Science series [37].

  Location: Section 5.4 presents the simulation framework.

- *Acquisition's complexity*

  Brief Description: Software acquisition projects are even more complex and risky than pure software development projects. This is at least what many people, specially project managers or consultants, feel when they deal with acquisition. A high-level system theoretic view on acquisition projects is presented which gives indicators for their higher complexity. This, or any similar view, did not exist in literature before – at least with respect to the author's knowledge. Parts of it are published at the International Workshop on Software Process Simulation Modeling 2003 (PROSIM'03) [35].

  Location: Section 1.2 (longer version) and section 7.4.2 (shorter version).

- *System Dynamics Design Methodology*

Brief Description: The current software process simulation literature does not treat the model design explicitly. In the author's opinion, there is a profound lack of research in design methodologies for system dynamic models of software processes. Model design is not treated explicitly in the respective literature which becomes specially eye-catching, when one tries to build models in a – with respect to System Dynamics – unexplored domain like software acquisition. An appropriate scientific approach is proclaimed and used. This is published at the International Workshop on Software Process Simulation Modeling 2003 (PROSIM'03) [35].

Location: Section 7.3 treats the approach and section 7.4 applies it.

- *A Framework for System Dynamics Models for Software Acquisition Projects*

  Brief Description: There are countless publications about system dynamics models of the software development process (or subprocesses of it like requirements management or testing); however, there are no attempts to model the software acquisition process described in literature. As part of this dissertation, the development of such a model together with the approach to develop it are described. The framework is additionally published at the International Workshop on Software Process Simulation Modeling 2003 (PROSIM'03) [35].

  Location: Section 7.4

- *A System Dynamics Model for Software Acquisition Projects*

  Brief Description: Based on the model framework treated in chapter 7, a fully quantified system dynamics model for a concrete software acquisition project is described. This model (like all system dynamics models of social systems) bases on many hypotheses. However all quantifications in this model (*unlike* in many comparable modeling projects unfortunately) are clearly justified and the respective hypotheses are explicated. This model is capable of reproducing the reference behavior modes, and it even helped the modeler (i.e. the author) to a deeper understanding of software acquisition dynamics; it fulfills its purposes and can, thus, be viewed as a valid model of the software acquisition process. The author plans to publish these results on the International Workshop on Software Process Simulation Modeling 2004.

Location: Section 8.3 and section 8.5

- *Combining Interactive Simulation with System Dynamics*

    Brief Description: An approach is described to combine the interactive simulation method treated in part II with the system dynamics concept. This is a step towards using the information which is coded in the System Dynamics model described in chapter 8 in an interactive simulation game.

    Location: Section 9.2

10.2. Imparting Knowledge in non-textbook style

This dissertation shows how to impart knowledge about the structure and the dynamics of software acquisition projects in non-textbook style.

It shows how to impart knowledge about the structure of a project through intelligently organizing high-level process and detailed best-practice knowledge in one coherent process model.

And it shows how to impart knowledge about the behavior of a software acquisition project through System Dynamics: it shows how to model the software acquisition process through System Dynamics and how to better understand the dynamics of software acquisition through that model.

10.3. Foundations for Building a Project Simulation Game

This dissertation presents an approach for the development of a software acquisition project simulation game, which uses a combination of two well-established description methods which sensibly complement one another: first, process description (in our case through the process description language HFSP) specifying the sequence of process steps which should ideally be performed in order in the respective project , and, second, system dynamics modeling, a method for specifying and simulating the behavior of a system.

This dissertation presents the process spectrum which could form the basis for the interactive simulation, it presents the a process-oriented interactive simulation methodology which could take the process as a basis, it presents a valid system dynamics model which describes the dynamics of software acquisition projects, and it finally describes a method to combine the process-oriented interactive simulation and System Dynamics.

Chapter 11

Outlook

Provided that we focus on the modeling and simulation techniques designed in this work and view the matter of "software acquisition" as a secondary issue, the work performed in this dissertation can be viewed under a different angle. Under these circumstances, we could rename the title to

"Techniques For Imparting Process Knowledge
(With Process Modeling, Interactive Simulation and System Dynamics)
Using the Software Acquisition Process as a Case Study"

That is, the techniques used and developed in this dissertation could be applied to other kinds of processes and process models; the work performed in this dissertation can be seen as a step towards better understanding of all kinds of processes. So, future work should deal with modeling and simulating other kinds of processes with the techniques described in this dissertation.

As aforementioned in chapter 10, this work's contribution can also be seen as the presentation of a fundament for a project simulation game. Under this perspective, we can see possible future work in developing and fully implementing a software acquisition project simulation game using the fundaments presented in this dissertation, and, possibly, in developing a spacial interactive simulation game (cf. section 5.7.3) using the techniques described in this dissertation.

Although all parts of this dissertation are self-contained and the research described is, in many senses, completed, we finally present open questions leading to further future work:

- Which programming techniques are most appropriate to implement a combination of System Dynamics with the process-oriented interactive simulation paradigm? Can the functional and higher-order programming paradigm be used in a similarly elegant way for the combination?

- The system dynamics framework described in section 7 should be applied to other types of software acquisition projects, to further test the validity and universality of the framework.

- Are there other reasonable techniques for interactive software process simulation?

- Are there other reasonable techniques – besides System Dynamics – that can be used to support the process-oriented interactive simulation technique in the description of the low-level dynamics? How smoothly are they integratable and how do they compare to System Dynamics?

Generally speaking, the research areas treated in this work offer the potential for a great gain of further knowledge. The systematic investigation in modeling and simulation of the software acquisition process is still in its early stages; this work is a first step.

Appendix A

Framework Implementation – The Sources

After shortly introducing the syntax of Vensim equations, this appendix presents the Vensim sources of the system dynamics model presented in chapter 8.

A.1. Syntax of the Equations

The following are the Vensim sources of the system dynamics model treated in chapter 8. Each equation corresponds to a level, rate, or auxiliary variable. Auxiliary and rate equations have the simple form:

$$identifier = term$$
$$\sim unit$$

Here, $identifier$ denotes the name of the respective variable, and $term$ prescribes its calculation rule. The modeler can additionally provide information about the unit of measure of the variable; the unit is separated from $term$ by a $\sim$-character.

The syntax is more complex, when the (rate or auxiliary) variable uses a table function for its calculation:

$$identifier = \texttt{WITH LOOKUP} \ (term, \ ([point_{min} - point_{max}], \ point, \ \dots \ ))$$
$$\sim unit$$

The input value to the table function is $term$. Separated by a comma follows the specification of the table function as a list of elements. The first element specifies the range (which is relevant for printing the table function): $point_{min}$ specifies the lower left corner and $point_{max}$ the upper right corner of the coordinate system in which the table function is printed. The remaining elements specify the table function's curve. The value of the variable *identifier* results from applying the table function to *term*.

The syntax of level variables differs from the syntax of rate or auxiliary variables:

$$identifier = \texttt{INTEG}\ (term_{integ},\ term_{ini})$$
$$\sim unit$$

Level variables are accumulations and they are treated as integrals in System Dynamics. The level equation means that the level variable has an initial value of $term_{ini}$ and Vensim integrates $term_{integ}$ to determine future values of the variable. The value of the level variable *identifier* at a given point in time $\tau \in [0, \texttt{FINAL TIME}]$ then calculates to

$$term_{ini} + \int_{t=0}^{\tau} term_{integ}\ dt$$

A.2. Model Sources

In the following, the complete sources of the Vensim model of a software acquisition project are presented. The form of most equations listed below is justified in detail in section 8.3.

```
%pressure=
Need for controlling and pressure
~ Dmnl

reported ratio = WITH LOOKUP (
QA execution rate,
([(0,0)-(0.2,1)],(0,1),(0.025,0.75),(0.065,0.5),(0.2,0.1) ))
~ Dmnl

Trust ratio=
MIN(1, Supplier's Trust*Supplier's Trust )
~ Dmnl

Supplier's Trust= INTEG (
MAX(-Supplier's Trust, Trust generation rate/100),
```

```
0.15)
~ Dmnl


QA generation rate=
MAX(0 , MIN(Maximum QA generation rate,
               (Need for controlling and pressure+
                Need for technical Know How)
               * 0.2 * Willingness for common QA
    ))*QA factor
~ Dmnl


QA execution rate=
MIN(Tasks for common QA activities ,
        MAX((Man Power for QA Activities /
              "actual Man-Days needed per QA task")
              * (Trust ratio),
              0))
~ QATask/Day


comm generation rate=
Nominal comm generation rate *
    (Need for controlling and pressure+Need for status information+
     Need for supplier support)
~ CommTask/Day


Reqs implemented= INTEG (
Supp's implementation rate,
0)
~ Req


Acq's Technological Knowledge=
Acquirer's experience*Knowledge Due to QA activities
~ Dmnl


Acquirer's experience=
0.4
~ Dmnl


Knowledge Due to QA activities = WITH LOOKUP (
QA Tasks Performed,
([(0,0)-(100,1)],(0,0.1),(25,0.5),(75,0.85),(100,0.9) ))
~ Dmnl


WF Level Sought=
```

```
MIN(Ceiling on New Hirees+Total Workforce, WF needed)
~ Man

Influence of pressure on comprehension = WITH LOOKUP (
(2*QA pressure+Comm pressure)/3,
([(0,0)-(1,2)],(0,0.75),(0.1,1.15),(0.25,1.3),(0.4,1.15),(0.5,0.5),
                    (0.7,0.3),(1,0.2)))
~

Influence of pressure on implementation = WITH LOOKUP (
(QA pressure+2*Comm pressure)/3,
([(0,0)-(1,2)],(0,0.7),(0.15,1.3),(0.3,1.5),(0.4,1.1),(0.5,0.5),
                    (0.7,0.35),(1,0.25)))
~

Comm pressure=
"%pressure"*communication execution rate*1.5
~ CommTask/Day

communication execution rate=
MIN(Tasks for regular communication,
        Man Power for Reg Comm/"actual Man-Days needed per comm. task")
~ CommTask/Day

QA pressure=
"%pressure"*QA execution rate*120
~ QATask/Day

Trust generation rate=
(Trust generation due to communication+Trust generation due to QA)*0.8
~ Dmnl/Day

Need for technical Know How=
(1-Acq's Technological Knowledge)*gap perceived
~ Dmnl

Need for supplier support=
 unclarity perceived*Multiplier to action due to time shortage
~ Dmnl

target progress=
Time/450
~ Dmnl
```

```
Total Requirements=
200
~ Req

Need for controlling and pressure=
MAX(0, (target progress-progress perceived)) *
         Multiplier to action due to time shortage
~ Dmnl

actual progress=
Reqs implemented/Total Requirements
~ Dmnl

Need for status information=
gap perceived
~ Dmnl

unclarity gap=
ABS(unclarity perceived-unclarity reported)/(unclarity perceived+0.001)
~ Dmnl

progress reported=
actual progress+(1-Trust ratio)*reported time factor*(1-actual progress)
~ Dmnl

unclarity reported=
actual unclarity-(1-Trust ratio)*reported time factor*actual unclarity
~ Dmnl

progress gap=
ABS(progress reported-progress perceived+0.01)/(progress perceived+0.01)
~ Dmnl

gap perceived=
(progress gap+unclarity gap)/2
~ Dmnl

Willingness for common QA = WITH LOOKUP (
Time Remaining,
([(0,0)-(500,1)],(0,0),(70,0),(125,0.25),(180,0.9),(320,1),(500,1) ))
~ Dmnl

Man Power for QA Activities=
Fraction of MP for QA Activities*Total Workforce
```

A. Framework Implementation – The Sources

~ Man

```
Fraction of MP for QA Activities=
Indicated WF level for QA Activities/
    (Indicated WF level for QA Activities+Indicated WF level for Reg Comm)
~ Dmnl
```

```
Man Power for Reg Comm=
(1-Fraction of MP for QA Activities)*Total Workforce
~ Man
```

```
Willingness to Change WF level = WITH LOOKUP (
(Hiring Delay+Average Assimilation Delay)/(Time Remaining+1),
([(0,0)-(2,1)],(0,1),(0.3,1),(1,0.2),(2,0)))
~ Dmnl
```

```
"Man-Days for Regular Communication"=
"actual Man-Days needed per comm. task"*Tasks for regular communication
~ Day*Man
```

```
"Man-Days for QA activities"=
"actual Man-Days needed per QA task"*Tasks for common QA activities
~ Day*Man
```

```
Max Delay in Regular Communication=
10
~ Day
```

```
Max Delay in QA Activities=
50
~ Day
```

```
Time Remaining=
500-Time
~ Day
```

```
Indicated WF level=
Indicated WF level for QA Activities+Indicated WF level for Reg Comm
~ Day
```

```
Indicated WF level for QA Activities=
"Man-Days for QA activities"/Max Delay in QA Activities
~ Man
```

```
Indicated WF level for Reg Comm=
"Man-Days for Regular Communication"/Max Delay in Regular Communication
~ Man

WF needed=
Willingness to Change WF level*Indicated WF level+
    (1-Willingness to Change WF level)*Total Workforce
~ Day

Total Workforce=
Experienced Workforce+0.5*Newly Hired Workforce
~ Man

WF Gap=
WF Level Sought-Total Workforce
~

Newly Hired Transfer Rate=
MIN(TRR, Newly Hired Workforce )
~ Man/Day

Newly Hired Workforce= INTEG (
+Hiring Rate-Assimilation Rate-Newly Hired Transfer Rate,
2)
~ Man

TRR=
MAX(0,- WF Gap/Transfer Delay )
~ Man/Day

reported time factor = WITH LOOKUP (
Time,
([(0,0)-(500,1)],(0,0),(125,0.25),(200,0.9),(300,1),(400,1),
                      (470,0.5),(500,0) ))
~ Dmnl

Ceiling on New Hires=
Experienced Workforce*Most New Hires Per Experienced Staff
~

Experienced Transfer Rate=
MIN(Experienced Workforce, TRR-Newly Hired Transfer Rate )
~ Man/Day
```

```
Experienced Workforce= INTEG (
Assimilation Rate-Experienced Transfer Rate-Quite Rate,
10)
~ Man

Assimilation Rate=
Newly Hired Workforce/Average Assimilation Delay
~ Man/Day

Average Assimilation Delay=
80
~ Day

Average Employment Time=
500
~ Day

Most New Hirees Per Experienced Staff=
3
~ Dmnl

Transfer Delay=
10
~ Day

Hiring Delay=
40
~ Day

Hiring Rate=
WF Gap/Hiring Delay
~ Man/Day

Quite Rate=
Experienced Workforce/Average Employment Time
~ Man/Day

progress perceived=
actual reported ratio*progress reported+(1-actual reported ratio) *
    actual progress
~ Dmnl

actual reported ratio=
reported ratio*(1-Acq's Technological Knowledge)
```

```
~ Dmnl


unclarity perceived=
actual reported ratio*unclarity reported+(1-actual reported ratio) *
    actual unclarity
~ Dmnl


Supp's implementation rate=
MIN(Reqs understood by Supplier,
        Influence of pressure on implementation * Unclarity Factor *
          (Basic impl rate+Impl from Tasks))
~ Req/Day


Daily ManPower for comm=
("actual Man-Days needed per comm. task" *
    Tasks for regular communication)/4
~ Man


Impl from Tasks=
5*QA execution rate
~


Multiplier to action due to time shortage = WITH LOOKUP (
Time,
([(0,0)-(500,1)],(0,0.25),(250,0.4),(325,0.7),(375,1),(500,1) ))
~ Dmnl


Basic impl rate=
0.6
~ Req/Day [0,2,0.05]


Unclarity Factor = WITH LOOKUP (
actual unclarity,
([(0,0)-(1,1)],(0,1),(0.25,0.9),(0.75,0.1),(1,0) ))
~ Dmnl


Reqs given to Supplier= INTEG (
Acquirer's comprehension rate-Supp's comprehension rate,
100)
~ Req


Comprehension from Tasks=
(1*QA execution rate + 0.2*communication execution rate) * 2
~ Dmnl
```

```
Reqs understood by Supplier= INTEG (
Supp's comprehension rate-Supp's implementation rate,
20)
~ Req

actual unclarity=
1 - ((Reqs understood by Supplier+Reqs implemented)/200)
~

Basic Comprehension=
0.5
~ Req/Day

Supp's comprehension rate=
MIN(Reqs given to Supplier,
        Influence of pressure on comprehension*(1-actual unclarity) *
        (Basic Comprehension+Comprehension from Tasks))
~ Req/Day

Acquirer's comprehension rate=
MIN(Requirements still not considered, 2*Acq's Technological Knowledge *
        littleness factor)
~ Req/Day

QA Tasks Performed= INTEG (
QA execution rate,
0)
~ QATask

Daily ManPower for QA=
(Tasks for common QA activities *
    "actual Man-Days needed per QA task") / 4
~ Man

Effectiveness in QA activities=
 Acq's Technological Knowledge
~ Dmnl

effectiveness in regular comm=
Acq's Technological Knowledge
~ Dmnl

littleness factor = WITH LOOKUP (
```

```
Requirements still not considered,
([[(0,0)-(100,1)],(0,0.1),(25,0.625),(50,0.875),(100,1)))
~


Nominal comm generation rate=
1
~ CommTask/Day

Maximum QA generation rate=
0.4
~ QATask/Day

policy for trust generation=
gap perceived
~ Dmnl

Trust generation due to QA = WITH LOOKUP (
"%pressure"*QA execution rate*10,
([[(0,-0.2)-(0.4,0.2)],(0,0.2),(0.05,0),(0.2,-0.15),(0.4,-0.2) ))
~ Dmnl

Trust generation due to communication = WITH LOOKUP (
"%pressure"*communication execution rate*6,
([[(0,-0.3)-(3,0.3)],(0,0.3),(0.3,0),(1,-0.2),(3,-0.3) ))
~

"Nominal Man-Days per QA task"=
10
~ Day*Man/QATask

"actual Man-Days needed per comm. task"=
(1/effectiveness in regular comm)*"nominal Man-Days per comm task"
~ Day*Man/CommTask

"actual Man-Days needed per QA task"=
(1.2 - Effectiveness in QA activities)*"Nominal Man-Days per QA task"
~ (Man*Day)/QATask

Tasks for common QA activities= INTEG (
+QA generation rate-QA execution rate,
5)
~ QATask

Tasks for regular communication= INTEG (
```

```
comm generation rate-communication execution rate,
15)
~ CommTask

"nominal Man-Days per comm task"=
0.5
~ Day*Man/CommTask

Requirements still not considered= INTEG (
-Acquirer's comprehension rate,
80)
~ Req

********************************************************
.Control
********************************************************~

Simulation Control Parameters
|

FINAL TIME  = 500
~ Day
~ The final time for the simulation.

INITIAL TIME  = 0
~ Day
~ The initial time for the simulation.

SAVEPER  =
        TIME STEP
~ Day [0,?]
~ The frequency with which output is stored.

TIME STEP  = 1
~ Day [0,?]
~ The time step for the simulation.
```

Bibliography

[1] Tarek Abdel-Hamid and Stuart E. Madnick. *Software Project Dynamics: An Integrated Approach.* Prentice Hall, Eaglewood Cliffs, New Jersey, 1991.

[2] Harold Abelson, Gerald Jay Sussman, and Julie Sussman. *Structure and Interpretation of Computer Programs.* MIT Press, Cambridge, Mass., second edition edition, 1996.

[3] Rembert Aranda, Thomas Fiddaman, and Rogelio Oliva. Quality microworlds: Modeling the impact of quality initiatives over the software product lifecycle. *American Programmer*, pages 52–61, 1993.

[4] Henk P. Barendregt. *Functional programming and lambda calculus*, volume B of *Handbook of Theoretical Computer Science – Formal Models and Semantics*, chapter 7. Elsevier Science Publishers, 1990.

[5] Gregory Bateson. *Steps to an Ecology of Mind.* Paladin Books, 1973.

[6] Barry W. Boehm. Software engineering. *IEEE Transactions on Computers*, 25(12):1226–1241, 1976.

[7] Barry W. Boehm. *Software Engineering Economics.* Prentice Hall, 1982.

[8] Barry W. Boehm, Bradford Clark, Ellis Horowitz, J. Christopher Westland, Raymond J. Madachy, and Richard W. Selby. Cost models for future software life cycle processes: COCOMO 2.0. *Annals of Software Engineering*, 1:57–94, 1995.

[9] Frederick P. Brooks. *The Mythical Man-Month: essays on software engineering. Anniversary edition with four new chapters.* Addison Wesley Longman, 1995.

[10] Aaron G. Cass, Barbara Staudt Lerner, Stanley M. Sutton, Eric K. McCall, Alexander E. Wise, and Leon J. Osterweil. Little-jil/juliette: A process definition language and interpreter. In *Proceedings of the International Conference on Software Engineering (ICSE)*, pages 754–758, Limerick, Ireland, 2000.

[11] Peter Cheeseman, James Kelly, Matthew Self, John Stutz, Will Taylor, and Don Freeman. AutoClass: A bayesian classification system. In *Machine Learning, Proceedings of the Fifth International Conference on Machine Learning*, pages 54–64, Ann Arbor, Michigan, USA, June 1988.

[12] S. James Choi and Walt Scacchi. Modeling and simulating software acquisition process architectures. *Journal of Systems and Software*, 59(3):343–354, 2001.

[13] Alan M. Christie and Mary Jo Staley. Organizational and social simulation of a software requirements development process. *Software Process: Improvement and Practice*, 5(2-3):103–110, 2000.

[14] C.F. Citro and E.A. Hanushek, editors. *The Uses of Microsimulation Modelling. Vol 1: Review and Recommendations.* National Academy Press, Washington, D.C., 1991.

[15] James S. Collofello, I. Rus, A. Chauhan, D. Houston, D. Sycamore, and D. Smith-Daniels. A system dynamics process simulator for staffing policies decision support. In *Hawaii International Conference on System Sciences (HICSS)*, January 1998.

[16] James S. Collofello, Zhen Yang, Derek Merrill, Ioana Rus, and John D. Tvedt. Modeling software testing processes. In *International Phoenix Conference on Computers and Communications (IPCCC'96)*, 1996.

[17] Jack Cooper and Matt Fisher. Software acquisition capability maturity model. Technical Report CMU/SEI-2002-TR-010, Software Engineering Institute, March 2002.

[18] Antony Courtney and Conal Elliott. Genuinely functional user interfaces. In *Proceedings of the 2001 ACM SIGPLAN Haskell Workshop*, Firenze, Italy, September 2001.

[19] Tom DeMarco and Timothy Lister. *Peopleware – Productive Projects and Teams.* Dorset House Publishing Company, February 1999.

[20] R. Kent Dybvig. *The Scheme Programming Language*. Prentice Hall, 1996.

[21] European Cooperation for Space Standardization (ECSS). *Space Engineering, Software*, 1998.

[22] Kiarash Fatehi. Modelling the impact of quality improvement initiatives. In *Proceedings of the International Conference on Software Engineering '98*, pages 164–165, Kyoto, Japan, April 1998.

[23] Kiarash Fatehi. *Planung von Prozessverbesserungen in Softwareentwicklungsprojekten unter Berücksichtigung qualitativer Informationen*. PhD thesis, Universität Ulm, November 1999.

[24] Federal Aviation Administration. *Integrated Capability Maturity Model*. http://www.faa.gov/aio/ProcessEngr/iCMM/.

[25] Robert Bruce Findler, John Clements, Cormac Flanagan, Matthew Flatt, Shriram Krishnamurthi, Paul Steckler, and Matthias Felleisen. Drscheme: a programming environment for scheme. *Journal of Functional Programming*, 12(2):159–182, 2002.

[26] Matthew Flatt. PLT MzScheme: Language manual. Technical report, Rice University, University of Utah, August 2003. Version 205.

[27] Matthew Flatt, Robert Bruce Findler, and John Clements. PLT MrEd: Graphical Toolbox Manual. Technical report, Rice University, University of Utah, August 2003. Version 205.

[28] Foldoc – free online dictionary of computing. http://foldoc.doc.ic.ac.uk.

[29] Jay W. Forrester. *Industrial Dynamics*. Productivity Press, Cambridge, Mass., London, 1961.

[30] Jay W. Forrester. *Principles of Systems*. Productivity Press, Cambridge, Mass., London, 1968.

[31] Jay W. Forrester. *World Dynamics*. Wright-Allen Press, Inc., Cambridge, Mass., 1971.

[32] Gerhard Getto. Evaluation von Prozessen und Methoden für Softwarebeschaffung und Management von Auftragnehmern. In *Proceedings of the 4th Kongress Software Qualitätsmanagement*, 1999.

[33] Gerhard Getto and Thomas Gantner. Software acquisition processes at DaimlerChrylser AG: Research activities for improvement. In *Proceedings of the European Conference on Software Process Improvement (SPI99)*, 1999.

[34] Nigel Gilbert and Klaus G. Troitzsch. *Simulation for the social scientist*, chapter 4. Open University Press – Buckingham – Philadelphia, 1999.

[35] Tobias Häberlein. A framework for system dynamic models of software acquisition projects. In *Proceedings of ProSim'03 (International Workshop on Software Process Simulation Modeling)*, Portland, Oregon, May 2003.

[36] Tobias Häberlein and Thomas Gantner. GARP – the evolution of a software acquisition process model. In J. Kontio and R. Conradi, editors, *Proceedings of the 7th European Conference on Software Quality 2002*, Lecture Notes in Computer Science 2349, pages 186–196. Springer-Verlag Heidelberg, 2002.

[37] Tobias Häberlein and Thomas Gantner. Process-oriented interactive simulation of software acquisition projects. In *Proceedings of the First Eurasian Conference on Advances in Information and Communication Technology*, Lecture Notes in Computer Science 2510, pages 806–815. Springer-Verlag Heidelberg, 2002.

[38] *Haskell 98, a non-strict, purely functional language.* http://www.haskell.org/definition, December 1998.

[39] Eric Horvitz, Jack S. Breese, David Heckerman, David Hovel, and Koos Rommelse. The Lumiere project: Bayesian user modeling for inferring the goals and needs of software users. In *UAI '98: Proceedings of the Fourteenth Conference on Uncertainty in Artificial Intelligence*, pages 256–265, University of Wisconsin Business School, Madison, Wisconsin, USA, 1998.

[40] John Hughes. Why functional programming matters. *Computer Journal*, 32(2):98–107, 1989.

[41] Watts S. Humphrey and Marc I. Kellner. Software process modeling: Principles of entity process models. In *Proceedings of the 11th International Conference on Software Engineering*, 1989.

[42] IEEE Standards Association. *IEEE 1062: IEEE Recommended Practice for Software Acquisition*, 1993.

[43] International Standards Organization (ISO) / International Electronical Commission (IEC). *Information technology Software life cycle processes*, 1995. ISO/IEC 12207:1995/FDAM.

[44] *ISPL: Information Service Procurement Library. Managing Acquisition Processes*, 1999.

[45] Takuya Katayama. A hierarchical and functional software process description and its enaction. In *Proceedings of the 11th International Conference on Software Engineering*, pages 343–352, 1989.

[46] Richard Kelsey, William Clinger, and Jonathan Rees. Revised[5] report on the algorithmic language Scheme. *Higher-Order and Symbolic Computation*, 11(1):7–105, 1998.

[47] Mary Cecelia Lacity and Rudy Hirschheim. *Information Systems Outsourcing: Myths, Metaphors and Realities*. John Wiley and Sons Ltd, April 1995.

[48] Reuven R. Levary and Chi Y. Lin. Modelling the software development process using an expert simulation system having fuzzy logic. *Software – Practice and Experience*, 21(2):133–148, February 1991.

[49] Jochen Ludewig. Modelle der Software-Entwicklung – Abbilder oder Vorbilder? *GI Softwaretechnik-Trends*, 9(3):1–12, October 1989.

[50] Jochen Ludewig and Marcus Deininger. Teaching software project management by simulation: The SESAM project. In Irish Quality Association, editor, *5th European Conference on Software Quality*, pages 417 – 426, Dublin, 1996.

[51] Ray Madachy and Denton Tarbet. Case studies in software process modeling with system dynamics. *Software Process: Improvement and Practice*, 5(2-3):133–146, 2000.

[52] Gordon E. McCray and T.D. Clark. Using system dynamics to anticipate the organizational impacts of outsourcing. *System Dynamics Review*, 15(4):345–373, 1999.

[53] Derek Merill and James Collofello. Improving software project management skills using a software project simulator. In *Frontiers in Education Conference*, 1997.

[54] B. Craig Meyers and Patricia Oberndorf. *Managing Software Acquisition: Open Systems and Cots*. SEI Series in Software Engineering. Addison Wesley Publishing Company, July 2001.

[55] Robin Milner, Mads Tofte, Robert Harper, and Dave Mac-Queen. *The Definition of Standard ML (Revised)*. MIT Press, 1997.

[56] The OpenGroup. *Beyond the Contract: An Analysis of the Business Impact of IT Procurement Best Practices*, 1999.

[57] Leon J. Osterweil. Software processes are software, too. In *Proceedings of the 9th International Conference on Software Engineering*, pages 2 – 13, 1987.

[58] Leon J. Osterweil. Modeling processes for effectively reasoning about their properties. In *Proceedings of the Process Simulation and Modelling Workshop*, Portland, Oregon, 2003.

[59] Helmuth Partsch. Folien zur Vorlesung "Softwaretechnik", 2003. Universität Ulm, Abteilung Programmiermethodik und Compilerbau.

[60] Dietmar Pfahl, Marco Klemm, and Günther Ruhe. Using system dynamics simulation models for software project management education and training. In *Proceedings of the 3rd Process Simulation Modeling Workshop*, London, UK, June 2000.

[61] Karl Popper. *The Logic of Scientific Discovery*. Hutchinson, 1959.

[62] Roger S. Pressman. *Software Engineering: a practitioner's approach*. McGraw-Hill, 2001.

[63] The Procurement Forum, Rond Point Schuman 6, B-1040 Brussels, Belgium. http://www.procurementforum.org.

[64] *PULSE: A Methodology for Assessment and Benchmarking of Procurement Processes*. http://archive.opengroup.org/sprite/pulse/index.htm.

[65] Juan F. Ramil and M. M. Lehman. Fuzzy dynamics in software project simulation and support. In *European Workshop on Software Process Technology*, pages 122–126, 1998.

[66] George P. Richardson and Alexander L. Pugh III. *System Dynamics Modeling with DYNAMO*. Productivity Press, Portland, Oregon, 1981.

[67] Kathy M. Ripin and Leonard R. Sayles. *Insider Strategies for Outsourcing Information Systems: Building Productive Partnerships, Avoiding Seductive Traps.* Oxford University Press, April 1999.

[68] Stephen T. Roehling, James S. Collofello, Brian G. Hermann, and Dwight E. Smith-Daniels. System dynamics modeling applied to software outsourcing decision support. *Software Process: Improvement and Practice,* 5(2-3):169–182, 2000.

[69] Esa Rosendahl and Ton Vullinghs. Performing initial risk assessment in software acquisition projects. In *Proceedings of the 7th European Conference on Software Quality,* 2002.

[70] W. W. Royce. Managing the development of large software systems. In *Proceedings of the 9th International Conference on Software Engineering,* pages 328–338, 1987. Originally published in the Proceedings of the WESCON Conference, 1970.

[71] Howard A. Rubin, Margaret Johnson, and Ed Yourdon. With the SEI as my copilot. Using software process flight simulation to predict the impact of improvements in process maturity. *American Programmer,* pages 50–57, September 1994.

[72] Howard A. Rubin, Margaret Johnson, and Ed Yourdon. Software process flight simulation. Dynamic modeling tools and metrics. *Information Systems Management,* summer 1995.

[73] Meurig Sage. FranTK – a declarative GUI language for Haskell. In *Proceedings of Fifth ACM SIGPLAN International Conference on Functional Programming (ICFP),* pages 106–117, Montreal, Canada, September 2000. ACM press.

[74] Walt Scacchi. Managing software engineering projects: A social analysis. *IEEE Transactions on Software Engineering,* 10(1), January 1984.

[75] Kurt Schneider. *Ausführbare Modelle der Software Entwicklung. Struktur und Realisierung eines Simulationssystems.* PhD thesis, Universität Stuttgart, 1994.

[76] Josef Schreiber. *Beschaffung von Informatikmitteln. Pflichtenheft, Evaluation, Entscheidung.* Paul Haupt Verlag, 2000.

[77] Simcity 4. http://www.SimCity.com, 2003.

[78] Software Engineering Coordinating Committee. *Guide to the Software Engineering Body of Knowledge (SWEBOK)*, May 2001. A Project of the IEEE Computer Society.

[79] Software Engineering Institute. *Software Acquisition Capability Maturity Model, Version 1.02*, cmu/sei-99-tr-002 edition, 2001.

[80] Software Productivity Consortium. *Process Definition and Modeling Guidebook*, 1992. SPC-92041-CMC.

[81] Software Program Managers Network. *Program Managers Guide to Software Acquisition*. http://www.spmn.com.

[82] Ian Sommerville. *Software Engineering*. Addison Wesley, 1982.

[83] John D. Tvedt. *An Extensible Model Evaluating the Impact of Process Improvements on Software Development Cycle Time*. PhD thesis, Arizona State University, 1996.

[84] Gerald M. Weinberg. *The psychology of computer programming*. Van Nostrand Reinhold, New York, 1971.

[85] Oliver E. Williamson. *Markets and Hierarchies: Analysis and Antitrust Implications. A Study in the Economics of Internal Organizations*. The Free Press, New York, 1975.

[86] Oliver E. Williamson. Transaction cost economics: The governance of contractual relations. *Journal of Law and Economics*, 22(2):233–261, October 1979.

[87] Helmut Willke. *Systemtheorie I: Grundlagen*. Lucius & Lucius Verlagsgesellschaft mbH Stuttgart, 2002.

[88] Massimo Zancanaro, Alessandro Cappelletti, Claudio Signorini, and Carlo Strapparara. An authoring tool for intelligent educational games. In *Proceedings of the International Conference on Virtual Storytelling*, Lecture Notes in Computer Science 2197, pages 61–68. Springer-Verlag Heidelberg, 2001.

Zusammenfassung

Seit nun mehr über 40 Jahren werden Softwareentwicklungsprozesse wissenschaftlich untersucht, und es gibt eine umfassende Literatur zu diesem Thema. Obwohl, wie einige Schätzungen sagen, fast ebensoviele Projekte die Beschaffung von Software zum Ziel haben, gibt es bis jetzt wenige wissenschaftliche Untersuchungen über Softwarebeschaffungsprozesse. Diese Arbeit beschäftigt sich mit *Softwareakquisition,* so nennen wir in dieser Arbeit die Beschaffung von maßgeschneideter – also eigens für den Auftraggeber entwickelter – Software. Viele Softwareakquisitionsprojekte scheitern. Grund ist deren oft unterschätzte Komplexität: In einer Softwareakquisition muss nämlich nicht nur die Arbeit der eigenen Mitarbeiter koordiniert werden, sondern es müssen – was vielleicht noch schwieriger ist – zwei oder sogar mehrere Projekte aufeinander abgestimmt werden.

Ziel dieser Arbeit ist die Entwicklung eines besseren Verständnisses für den Ablauf von Softwareakquisitionsprojekten und auch die Untersuchung von Prozessmodellierungs- und Prozesssimulationstechniken, die dieses Verständnis erleichtern. Wir verwenden sowohl etablierte Techniken, wie die Modellierung und Simulation mit System Dynamics, als auch im Rahmen dieser Dissertation neu entwickelte Techniken, wie die Prozessmodellarchitektur "GARP", die prozessorientierte interaktive Simulation und eine Kombination aus interactiver Simulation mit System Dynamics.

Teil I: Prozessmodellierung. Der erste Teil dieser Dissertation beschäftigt sich mit der statischen Modellierung des Softwareakquisitionsprozesses in dem workflowähnlichen Prozessmodell GARP. Dieses Prozessmodell beinhaltet eine umfangreiche Sammlung an Wissen über Softwareakquisitionsprozesse. Es ist speziell auf die Bedürfnisse von Prozessberatern von Akquisitionsprojekten zugeschnitten. Sein Aufbau unterscheidet sich von anderen statischen Modellen des Akquisitionprozesses (wie beispielsweise PULSE oder SA-CMM): die einzelnen Prozessschritte sind – soweit möglich – zeitlich geordnet, sie decken möglichst alle denkbaren Arten von Softwareakquisitionsprojekten ab, und zusätzlich sind Informationen über konkrete Umsetzungsmöglichkeiten der Prozessschritte ins Modell integriert. Wir beschreiben die Architektur und die Anwendungen von GARP.

Teil II: Prozessorientierte Interaktive Simulation. Teil I ist die Basis für Teil II, der eine neuartige Technik der Prozesssimulation beschreibt. Diese Technik erlaubt es, GARP – aber auch andere ähnlich geartete Prozessmodelle – so direkt wie möglich auf eine *interaktive* Simulation abzubilden. Unter "interaktiver Simulation" verstehen wir eine Spielsimulation; in unserem Fall übernimmt der Spieler darin die Rolle des Projektmanagers. Im Gegensatz zu den bisher in der Literatur beschriebenen interaktiven Simulationstechniken, hat unser Ansatz einen Prozess als Grundlage. Er wurde unter Verwendung von Techniken aus der funktionalen Programmierung entwickelt, die es erlauben, Prozessschritte elegant miteinander zu verknüpfen.

Die beschriebene prozessorientierte interaktive Simulation ist generisch: Sie abstrahiert von der detaillierten Beschreibung der Feindynamik. Zur genauen Beschreibung der Feindynamik eignet sich beispielsweise System Dynamics.

Teil III: Modellierung und Simulation mit System Dynamics. System Dynamics wird zwar schon über längere Zeit zur Modellierung und Simulation der Dynamik von Sofware*entwicklungs*projekten eingesetzt, es wurde aber noch nie versucht – zumindest gibt es keine entsprechenden Publikationen –, die Dynamik von Softwareakquisitionsprojekten durch System Dynamics zu simulieren. Das vorgestellte Material ist entsprechend neuartig.

Wir halten Strukturen, die allen systemdynamischen Modellen des Softwareakquisitionsprozesses gemeinsam sind, in einem systemdynamischen "Framework" fest. Dieses "Framework" wird auf seine Allgemeingültigkeit und Validität hin untersucht. Wir entwickeln dann, anhand dieses Frameworks, ein systemdynamisches Modell für ein konkretes Akquisitionsprojekt. Schließlich wird die Validität dieses Modells untersucht.

Teil IV: Kombination der interaktiven Simulation mit System Dynamics. Der vierte Teil präsentiert einen Ansatz die im zweiten Teil beschriebene prozessorientierte interaktive Simulation mit System Dynamics zu kombinieren.

Diese Arbeit als Ganzes und ihre Ergebnisse können unter mehreren Blickwinkeln gesehen werden:

- Als ein allmähliches Herantasten an eine möglichst vollständige Sicht auf die Softwareakquisition, angefangen von einem rein statischen hin zu einem dynamischen und interaktiven Blickwinkel.

- Als die Untersuchung von Methoden und Techniken, Wissen über Softwareprozesse in nicht-textueller Form zu vermitteln.

- Als die Präsentation der Grundlagen, die nötig sind, um ein Simulationsspiel für Softwareakquisitionsprojekte zu bauen.